Uncle John's
BATHROOM PUZZLER
365
LOGIC PUZZLES

D1417117

PORTABLE
PRESS

Bathroom Readers' Institute
Ashland, Oregon, and San Diego, California

Uncle John's Bathroom Puzzler
365 Logic Puzzles

Copyright © 2008 by Portable Press. All rights reserved.
No part of this book may be used or reproduced
in any manner whatsoever without written permission,
except in the case of brief quotations embodied
in critical articles or reviews.

"Bathroom Reader," "Portable Press," and
"Bathroom Readers' Institute" are registered trademarks
of Baker & Taylor, Inc. All rights reserved.

For information, write
The Bathroom Readers' Institute
P.O. Box 1117, Ashland, OR 97520
www.bathroomreader.com
E-mail: mail@bathroomreader.com

ISBN 13: 978-1-59223-884-2
ISBN 10: 1-59223-884-X

Printed in Canada
First printing: December 2008

08 09 10 11 12   10 9 8 7 6 5 4 3 2 1

Thank You!

The Bathroom Readers' Institute sincerely thanks
the following people whose advice, assistance,
and hard work made this book possible.

Gordon Javna
JoAnn Padgett
Melinda Allman
Stephanie Spadaccini
Maggie McLaughlin
Jacqueline Damian
Jeff Altemus
Rob Davis
Julia Papps
Angela Kern
Amy Miller
Dan Mansfield
Sydney Stanley
Kait Fairchild
Monica Maestas
Lisa Meyers
Amy Ly
Ginger Winters
Jennifer Frederick
Cynthia Francisco
Julie, Elise, and Transcontinental

LOGICALLY SPEAKING

Here at the Bathroom Readers' Institute, we like to keep our brains in tip-top shape by quizzing each other: for example, if a rodeo stars six cowboys, one who is a dentist and another who rides a horse named Trigger, what is each guy's job and where did he place in the competition? (More clues on page 16.) So when it came time to develop our next Bathroom Puzzler, Uncle John encouraged us to put those skills to work. After all, he told us, remember what Leonard Nimoy once said: "Logic is the beginning of wisdom."

Puzzle Power!

We started researching right away and discovered two things: 1) a puzzle a day keeps the brain cells sharp, and 2) the word "logic" comes from the Greek term *logos*, meaning "reason." So we got to work, searching for puzzles that required reason to solve, and we decided to include a total of 365—so you, fearless reader, could do one a day and keep your brain brawny. Here's what we came up with:

• **Traditional logic puzzles:** These offer a set of clues and ask you to wade through what's true and what isn't to match up people, places, events, and so on.

• **Word ladders:** Author Lewis Carroll invented the word game we now call "word ladders," in which the object is to change one word into another by changing one letter at a time, using the fewest steps possible. For example, MORE becomes LESS in four steps: MORE, LORE, LOSE, LOSS, LESS. (No proper nouns allowed, by the way.)

• **Mysteries:** We called on the BRI's favorite private eye, Inspector Commodius Loo, to investigate some crimes. See if you come up with the same outcomes he does.

• **Wild & Woolly Wordies:** These are visual word puzzles, like "cross-stitch":

$$
\begin{array}{ccccc}
 & & S & & \\
 & & T & & \\
S & T & I & T & C & H \\
 & & T & & \\
 & & C & & \\
 & & H & &
\end{array}
$$

• **Echoes:** These puzzles include homophones, words that sound alike but are spelled differently and mean different things—like "two" and "too."

• **Cryptograms**, anagrams, hidden messages...and even a few surprises.

So now, with your thinking cap pulled on tight and your logic skills at the ready, we wish you good luck and happy puzzling.

—Uncle John and the BRI Staff

1. HIGH SCHOOL REUNION

Four former friends attended their 10th high school reunion. From the following statements, can you figure out each woman's full name, high school claim to fame, and current occupation?

1. Neither Heather nor French was voted Most Likely to Succeed or selected as valedictorian.

2. Zoe and Sophie still live in the same town as their high school; Moskowitz lives in another state.

3. Mayer, who isn't Zoe, is a computer programmer.

4. The dentist was voted Class Clown; the one with the Most School Spirit is a financial consultant.

5. Mulroney and Binky both had to travel a significant distance to attend the reunion.

6. The lawyer (who was not voted Most Likely to Succeed), Heather, and the financial consultant went to the same college.

Here's a sample grid to get you started:

	Surname	**Claim to Fame**	**Occupation**
Sophie			
Heather			
Binky			
Zoe			

2. CONNECT THE STARS

How many squares can you make by connecting any four stars? (Note: The corners of a square have to be on a star.)

3. GONE FISHIN'

Eddie and his three best buddies went fishing and caught six fish total. One of them caught three, another caught two, one caught one, and one didn't catch any. Match each guy with the fish he did or didn't catch, and figure out what each used for bait.

1. The guy who caught two fish wasn't Adam or the one who used worms.

2. The one who used the bologna didn't catch as many as Roberto.

3. Dry flies worked the best; the guy who used them caught the three fish.

4. Oscar used bacon.

5. Adam didn't use the bologna.

4. WHAT'S THE WORD?

Can you think of a word that can be placed in front of each set of five words to form new words or phrases? For example, if the words were: CAKE, DOG, FOOT, HEAD, STUFF, you could add HOT to get HOTCAKE, HOT DOG, HOTFOOT, HOTHEAD, and HOT STUFF. Now you try it:

DISTANCE, JUMP, HORN, BOW, WINDED

Q: What did the nuclear physicist have for lunch? (A: Fission chips.)

5. INSPECTOR LOO AND THE BUMBLING ARCHAEOLOGIST

Famous inspector Commodius Loo looked up from his Guinness at a swaggering fellow in safari garb across the bar. Christopher "Kansas" Katz was regaling the regulars at Loo's favorite dive with his adventures as an archaeologist.

"So, then I heard about a lost village, a half-buried ghost town in the wilds of West Chaluchistan," Kansas said. "No archaeologist had ever set foot there, but I convinced one of the locals to guide me."

"What did pay him, bro?" a customer called out. The rest of the group laughed.

"A thousand bucks," Kansas said. "But that's chump change, considering what we found."

He pulled a gold coin encased in a plastic sleeve out of his pocket.

"Take a look," he said, passing the coin around the bar. "I've got a couple dozen more locked up in a safe. See? The date's stamped here, along the rim. It says 337 BC. in the ancient local language. There's no prior record of coins being minted in West Chaluchistan so early."

The coin came to Loo. He took a quick look, then cocked one bushy ginger eyebrow.

"Bogus," he pronounced, handing the coin back to Kansas. "You've been rooked."

How did Inspector Loo know the coin was fake?

6. TODAY'S THE DAY!

If today is Monday, what is the day after the day before the day before tomorrow?

7. WHAT HAPPENS IN VEGAS

Three couples recently visited Las Vegas. The men—Harry, Bernard, and Oswald—and the women—Belinda, Betty, and Vera—each gambled independently, but agreed to stop whenever each couple's gain or loss reached $200. All three husbands lost money, but each couple won exactly $200. Bernard lost $504 more than Harry. Betty won $2,376 more than Vera. Who is married to whom?

8. WILD & WOOLLY WORDY

Can you figure out what word or phrase these stand for?

CHIMADENA

In 1738, a Frenchman created a mechanical duck that could eat, flap its wings, and poop.

9. CRIMINOLOGY

Five of the students in Professor Shirley Kay Holmes's criminology class were suspects in the theft of the professor's magnifying glass. Each student made three statements, two of which were true and one of which was false. Can you sift through the evidence and nail the thief?

Nero:
> **1.** I didn't take the magnifying glass.
> **2.** I've never stolen anything.
> **3.** Nora did it.

Jane:
> **4.** I didn't take the magnifying glass.
> **5.** I have my own magnifying glass.
> **6.** Sam knows who did it.

Nick:
> **7.** I didn't take the magnifying glass.
> **8.** I didn't know Sam before I enrolled in this class.
> **9.** Nora did it.

Nora:
> **10.** I am not guilty.
> **11.** Sam did it.
> **12.** Nero is lying when he says I stole the magnifying glass.

Sam:
> **13.** I didn't take the magnifying glass.
> **14.** Jane is guilty.
> **15.** Nick and I are old friends.

Who stole the magnifying glass?

Pea brain? The average human brain weighs 1,400 grams...

10. DINNER'S ON!

A mother has four hungry children and only three potatoes. Without using fractions, can you figure out how she
can feed all of them, serving them each an equal amount
of potatoes?

11. ACEY-DEUCEY

Eight cards (all aces and deuces) are dealt, with every second card being returned to the bottom of the pack. That
means that the first card goes faceup on the table, the
second card goes to the bottom of the pack, the third goes
on the table to the right of the first card, and so on, until
all the cards are dealt.

Here's what the cards on the table look like:

A 2 A 2 A 2 A 2

Can you figure out how the cards were originally stacked?

...Albert Einstein's weighed only 1,230 grams.

12. SUMMER AT CAMP MANY-HAHAS

The camp counselors are discussing three campers who are due to arrive the next day. Looking at the list, one of them says, "Bernstein, Garcia, and Klein arrive tomorrow. Their first names are Katie, Peter, and Gracie, but not necessarily in that order."

"I think Katie's last name is Bernstein," said another counselor.

"No, that's wrong," said the first counselor. "I'll give you a few hints. Garcia is one year older than Peter, Gracie is older than Garcia, and Bernstein is the oldest of the three."

If this is the fifth year at the camp for all three and Peter has been coming to the camp since he was seven, what are the first and last names of the three campers, and their ages?

13. QUICK TRICK

If 8 - 22 - 5 - 22 - 13 = 7, and 7 - 4 - 12 = 2, how would you write 10?

14. TRIPLETS

See if you can figure out the relationship between the numbers in each of the first three sets of numbers, and then apply that to the last three sets to fill in the blanks.

2 5 10
3 10 20
4 17 34
5 __ __
__ 37 __
__ __ 100

15. WORD GAME

Can you name four days that start with the letter T?

16. IT'S SYMBOLIC

This message is trying to tell you something. Can you figure out what it is?

17. COMPARING APPLES & SISTERS

Eight children divided 32 apples as follows: Angela got one, Marcy two, Janette three, and Kristen four. Norbert Smythe took as many as his sister, Tristan Brownfield took twice as many as his sister, Bart Jackson took three times as many as his sister, and Jed Redfield took four times as many as his sister.

What are the girls' last names?

First $1 million winner on *Who Wants to Be a Millionaire*: IRS agent John Carpenter.

18. DEAR OLD DAD

When my father was 30, I was 7. Now he's twice as old as I am. How old am I?

19. WILD & WOOLLY WORDY

Can you figure out what word or phrase these stand for?

S
L
O
W

20. WHERE THERE'S A WILL...

Old Aunt Leticia was a generous soul. In her will, she left $666,666 to two fathers and two sons, to be split equally. They all walked away with $222,222. How was this possible?

21. INSPECTOR LOO AND THE STRANGER

International man of mystery Inspector Commodius Loo was sitting in his hotel room in Cleveland, oiling his gun, when he heard someone knock on the door and then insert a key card into the lock. Inspector Loo went over and opened the door.

"Yo, sorry, my man!" said the stranger as he took in all of Loo's six feet, six inches. "I thought this was my room. I must have gotten off on the wrong floor. They all look identical, don't they?"

The stranger laughed weakly and gave a little wave of the hand as he made his way to the elevator.

The inspector closed the door and went right to the phone to alert the front desk that a thief was stalking the halls.

How did Loo know the stranger was up to no good?

22. THE SAME GAME

What do the following items have in common?

Skis, Chopsticks, Windshield wipers, Knitting needles, Dice

Benjamin Franklin never patented any of his inventions.

23. OINK, OINK, OUCH!

You've just smashed open your piggy bank to discover 55 coins totaling $10.00. If there are more nickels than pennies, more dimes than nickels, and more quarters than dimes, how many of each coin do you have?

24. CHOO-CHOO!

Take a look at this equation:

```
  C H O O
+ C H O O
---------
T R A I N
```

If TRAIN = 12954, what four numbers equal CHOO?

25. MYSTERY MATH

Can you arrange sixteen 4s so that they add up to 1,000?

The New York Times and its journalists have won a record 91 Pulitzer prizes.

26. WHAT'S THE WORD?

Can you think of a word that can be placed in front of each set of five words to form five new words or phrases? For example, if the words were: CAKE, DOG, FOOT, HEAD, STUFF, you could add HOT to get HOTCAKE, HOT DOG, HOTFOOT, HOTHEAD, and HOT STUFF. Now you try it:

TABLE, UP, TAIL, PIKE, OVER

27. HERE'S LOOKING AT YOU, KID

Jan and Jill ran into each other at a reunion. They hadn't seen one another since their school days. "Good grief," Jan told Jill, "you must have gained a hundred pounds!"

Jill was not overweight. So, why was Jan's estimate accurate?

28. RAPID FIRE

• You're running in a marathon (good for you!), and you overtake the person in second place. What position are you in now?

• If you started spelling out numbers (one, two, three, and so on), how far would you have to go until you found the letter A?

The average score on an IQ test is 100.

29. TRICKY TRIANGLES

Calculate the missing number.

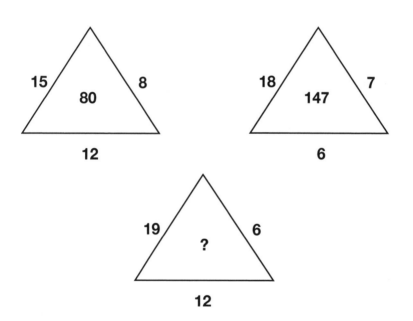

The *Star Trek* character Q had an IQ of 2005.

30. RODEO ROUNDUP

Six brave (or foolhardy) guys competed in the amateur cattle-roping event at this year's annual Round-Em-Up Rodeo. From the clues below, can you figure out where each one placed in the competition, his occupation, and the name of his horse?

1. Wes Podunk finished immediately ahead of the dentist, whose horse is Kickapoo; the dentist is not Steve Burly.

2. Jake Slaughter's mount is Dusty; Jake did not finish in first or last place.

3. The florist finished in an even-numbered position.

4. Moose Jessup, who isn't a newspaper editor, came in second; Duke Washburton finished two places ahead of the man riding Goldie.

5. Factory foreman Rusty Canter finished immediately ahead of Pardner and his rider, the florist.

6. The competitor who came in fourth is a radio show host.

7. The corporate lawyer didn't ride Trigger.

8. The man who finished in third place rode a horse called Arbuckle.

"No one will ever need more than 640K of RAM." —*Bill Gates*

31. A SAFE PLACE

Fred leaves home, but when he tries to return, a man wearing a mask is blocking his path. What is Fred doing, and what is the masked man's occupation?

32. MADE IN THE USA

Which of the following isn't a state?

> STAEX
> IHGCCOA
> GOYIWMN
> IMENA

33. SOCK IT TO ME

Mr. Rose, Mr. Olive, and Mr. Ivory work together in the men's department at Boomingsales. They showed up at work today wearing socks that match the colors of their last names—although no man's socks matches his own name. Mr. Rose didn't wear the olive socks. What is the color of each man's socks?

H. G. Wells theorized atomic energy in his 1914 novel *The World Set Free*.

34. IT FIGURES

What should come next in this series?

35. THE INSPECTOR SOLVES A KIDNAPPING CASE

T om Travail called Inspector Commodius Loo because he didn't want to call the police. His son Tony had been kidnapped, and the midnight drop of half a million dollars hadn't gone as planned. Tony was still missing and his twin, Terry—who had delivered the gym bag full of cash—was nursing a bump on the head.

"I went to the deserted parking garage like they told me," Terry told the inspector, "when somebody conked me on the back of the head. I fell and dropped the gym bag. My attacker swooped down from behind me, picked it up, and ran off. I never saw his face, only his back. He was tall and red-headed, wearing chinos and a zippered sweatshirt—it might have had a college logo, I couldn't quite see in the dark."

"Anyone else around?" Loo asked.

"A homeless guy showed up pushing a shopping cart," Terry said. "Then someone drove up in a Mercedes. He wanted to call the cops, but I begged him not to—the kidnappers said no police."

"Now they want another half million," Tom wailed. "What should we do? Should we interrogate the homeless man and Mercedes driver?"

"No need," Loo said. "I know what happened."

How and what did Inspector Loo know?

IBM currently holds more than 40,000 U.S. patents.

36. WONDERFUL WORDPLAY

In the brackets, write the word that means the same (in one sense) as the word on its left and (in another sense) the same as the word on its right.

Dash [_ _ _ T] Missile

Contest [_ A _ _ _] Equal

Ignite [_ I _ _] Shoot

37. I'LL TAKE ROMANCE

Three romance novels are on a shelf, lined up from left to right. Can you tell from the clues what the title of each book is, who wrote it, and the color of its cover?

1. The purple book is farther to the left than the one written by Barbara Musk, but farther right than the book *Long Nights*.

2. The book by Rosamund Fahrquar is to the right of the puce book. One of the books has a fuchsia cover.

3. Danielle Skweel's book is next to *Shining Armor*. One of the books is entitled *Heart on Fire*.

Sports cause about 300,000 concussions every year.

38. LOGIC BY THE NUMBERS

To solve this one, you'll need only a glancing familiarity with math—this one can be solved mostly by logic. There's a two-digit number that, when read from right to left, is 4½ times as large as from left to right. Can you figure out what it is? Here are some hints if you get stuck:

- The number is greater than 9 because it has two digits.

- The number is less than 23 because 23 x 4½ is greater than 100 (a three-digit number).

- The number is an even number because multiplying an odd number by 4½ will produce a fraction or decimal.

- Half the number times 9 is its reverse, so its reverse is divisible by 9.

Studies show: People with lower IQs are at greater risk of getting a concussion.

39. THE LUNCHTIME CROWD

Lunchtime at DeeDee's Diner was so crowded that four strangers had to sit together at one table. Each ordered a sandwich, one side dish, and a dessert, but everyone ordered something different. From these clues, can you figure out the full name of each person and what he had for lunch?

1. Peter Waller didn't have coleslaw with his sandwich, which wasn't roast beef. The man who had the rice pilaf also had chocolate cake.

2. Mr. Benjamin, whose first name isn't Marco, didn't order the garden salad or the marionberry pie. Walter didn't order a tofu sandwich or baked potato.

3. Emlyn thought the hot-fudge sundae looked a lot better than his dessert, but agreed that his side dish looked a lot better than Marco's salad.

4. Mr. Hanks and Peter didn't order a dessert with ice cream. Emlyn didn't order the baked potato, though he did get the turkey sandwich.

5. The man who got green-tea ice cream, and it wasn't Walter, ordered coleslaw with his sandwich.

6. Mr. Wayvern, whose first name isn't Walter, ordered a Spam sandwich but didn't order marionberry pie.

Child prodigy John von Neumann told jokes in classical Greek...at age 6.

40. THE MAGIC NUMBER

Here's a math trick from Uncle John. Try it out on your friends:

1. Ask someone to think of a number between 1 and 100, and to keep it a secret.

2. Using a calculator, take your age, multiply by 2, add 5, multiply by 50, and subtract 365.

3. Keeping that number on the calculator, hand the calculator to your victim, and tell him or her to add the secret number, and then add 115.

4. Voilà! The first half of the resulting number is your age, and the other part of the number is your friend's secret number!

41. RAPID FIRE

• What word, if pronounced "right," is wrong, but if pronounced "wrong" is right?

• Divide 30 by one half and add 10. What is the answer?

• How many 41-cent stamps are there in a dozen?

There is an infinite number of prime numbers.

42. THINK ABOUT IT

What is the significance of a carrot, a pile of pebbles, and a pipe lying together in the middle of a field?

43. WHAT'S THE WORD?

Here's a classic little verse that spells out a word, letter by letter. "My first" (and so on) refers to the mystery word's first letter. Can you figure out what word is being described?

> My first is in fish but not in snail.
>
> My second is in rabbit but not in tail.
>
> My third is in up but not in down.
>
> My fourth is in tiara not in crown.
>
> My fifth is in tree you plainly see.
>
> My whole is a food for you and me.

44. WILD & WOOLLY WORDY

Can you figure out what word or phrase this stands for?
THEAWALKPARK

National Spelling Bee winning word in 2008: guerdon.

45. IT'S HISTORY

Arthur O'Connor, an 18th-century Irish military man, wrote the following while in prison:

> The pomps of Courts and pride of kings
> I prize above all earthly things;
> I love my country, but the king,
> Above all men, his praise I sing.
> The Royal banners are displayed,
> And may success the standard aid.
>
> I fain would banish far from hence.
> The 'Rights of Man' and 'Common Sense'
> Confusion to his odious reign,
> That foe to princes, Thomas Paine.
> Defeat and ruin seize the cause.
> Of France, its liberties and laws.

If you read the verse in a different way, you'll discover a completely different meaning to it.

46. GETTING AWAY WITH MURDER

A man witnessed the murder of his girlfriend by his brother. It was an open-and-shut case. There were no police errors or procedural problems. Yet the judge decreed it was impossible to punish the offender. Why?

Lisa Simpson's IQ is 159; Homer's is 55.

47. GREEN, GREEN GRASS

Changing one letter at a time, can you go from GRASS to GREEN in seven steps?

48. A WEIGHTY PROBLEM

Back in his dieting days, Jim had three bathroom scales at home, but he obviously hasn't used them in years. The last time he weighed in at his doctor's office, he tipped the scales at a whopping 425 pounds. The doctor put him on a strict diet, with instructions to weigh himself every day—but the problem is his bathroom scales only go up to 250 pounds. How can Jim weigh himself accurately at home?

49. GO FIGURE

Can you make the following equation correct?

$$8 + 8 = 91$$

The first known written numbers appear on a Sumerian clay tablet from 3000 BC.

50. THE POWER OF 9

Ask someone to secretly write down any number that's at least four digits long. Let's say they choose 56832. Now ask that person to add up the digits, in this case, 5+6+8+3+2 = 24, then subtract the answer from the first number (56832 – 24 = 56808). Next, ask the person to cross out any one digit from the answer except a zero and then read you the new number. Let's say the 6 was crossed out, so the number now is 5808.

Even though you haven't seen any of the numbers, you can tell the person the number that was just crossed out. They'll be amazed when you say "Six."

(Check out the answer pages to see how it works.)

51. FAMILY RELATIONSHIPS

Charlotte is Mitzi's daughter's aunt's husband's daughter's sister. What's the relationship between Charlotte and Mitzi?

52. CAPITAL PUN-ISHMENT

The clues below are puns on particular words or phrases. The numbers in parentheses give you a hint: they refer to the number of letters in the answer; for example, "helping hand" would be (7,4).

Die of the cold? (3,4)

53. LETTER PERFECT

Fill in the blanks to make the sentence true.

In this sentence there are ___ O's, ___ T's, and ___ N's.

54. LO-CAL PIES

Four judges (including Bebe) at the Picky Eaters Food Institute tried out four low-calorie pies last week. Because one of the judges was allergic to coconut, they sliced the four pies this way:

- 3 coconut pie slices
- 5 blueberry pie slices
- 4 pecan pie slices
- 4 lemon meringue slices

Using the clues below, figure out which judge ate which kinds of pie, and how many slices of each.

Note: All four judges had four slices total.

1. Only two of the judges tested one of each kind.

2. No one ate more than three slices of any one kind.

3. Hortense tested one coconut and one lemon meringue.

4. Patrice tested three of one kind; her fourth was lemon meringue.

5. Two of the judges tasted one of each kind.

6. Jeanmarie didn't try the blueberry pie.

If stretched out, your cerebral cortex would be about the size of a bath mat.

55. INSPECTOR LOO AND THE CASE OF THE COLUMNIST

Commodius Loo gazed around the cluttered office where the Internet gossip columnist Mack Ronin had been fatally stabbed. Mack's assistant, Roger, discovered the body that morning when he reported to work, and the cops had immediately called Loo.

The famed detective found there were numerous suspects. A lot of people had a bone to pick with Mack, starting with his ex-wife Kayla Keir, the sexy singer whose career Mack had tried to sabotage after their divorce. Next was Mack's girlfriend, the solid-waste heiress Alicia Alto, who—according to Roger—had threatened to call Daddy when Mack refused to marry her. (Daddy was said to be connected.)

After them came a line of stars and wannabes whom Mack had slandered in his scandalous—but widely read—blog.

Mack's body was draped over his computer keyboard. Inspector Loo moved the mouse to bypass Mack's screen saver of frolicking puppies, and the dead man's final article—about Kayla and her new squeeze—popped into view. At the bottom of the file appeared a line of apparent gibberish: "49t34 w5qgg3e j3."

The cops asked if they should call the suspects in for questioning, but the inspector told them to arrest Roger. How did he ID the killer?

56. WHAT'S THE SCOOP?

Congratulations on your new job as head scooper at
Gino's Gelato. The tubs of gelato in front of you are labeled
from left to right as follows: CHOCOLATE, VANILLA,
BERRY-BERRY, HAZELNUT, and COCONUT. But the
scooper you're replacing was fired because he'd mislabeled
all the tubs. In fact, if the labels were moved around so
that the tubs were correctly labeled, no label would end
up next to a label that it started out next to. Given the fact
that the middle jar doesn't contain the chocolate, you'd
better figure out which labels belong on which tubs—the
shop is about to open.

57. WILD & WOOLLY WORDY

Can you figure out what word or phrase these stand for?

R
O
R A I L
D

58. SEQUENTIAL THINKING

In the following sequence, what number comes after 66?

2, 4, 6, 30, 32, 34, 36, 40, 42, 44, 46,
50, 52, 54, 56, 60, 62, 64, 66 . . .

59. COINS OF THE REALM

Congratulations! You've just been elected treasurer of the National Coin Repository. You'll be able to undertake your new duties as soon as you figure out how many coins are in the treasury. Trouble is, the coin counters, each of whom counts one type of coin, had been hoping that they'd get your job, so they aren't going to make it easy on you.

When you ask how many coins each of them has in his subtreasury, they'll only give you a statement about the numbers of coins in the other two subtreasuries. The gold coin counter says there are 3,000 silver and 5,000 bronze coins; the silver coin counter says there are 3,000 gold and 5,000 bronze; the bronze coin counter says there are 4,000 gold and 3,000 silver. The only thing you know is that there are 12,000 coins altogether.

If only one coin counter was telling the truth, and if each of the other two was lying about at least one amount, how many of each type were there?

The word "sophomore" is a combination of Greek words meaning "wise fool."

60. INSPECTOR LOO OUTWITS A DEAD MAN

A group of heirs—the nieces and nephews of a miserable old man who had just died—placed an emergency call to super sleuth Commodius Loo. Uncle Murray Mayo had played one final trick on them all.

Rather than divide his considerable estate among them, as they had every right to expect, the old geezer had instructed his executor to liquidate all assets after his death and place the money in his coffin. The coffin and its contents, he ordered, should then be cremated.

The family begged Inspector Loo to convince the executor to ignore Uncle Murray's orders or, failing that, to recommend another course of action.

Obviously, speed was of the essence—Murray's body had to be disposed of sooner rather than later—so a drawn-out court battle wasn't an option.

Loo determined from the executor that the old man was of sound mind when he issued his final instructions.

Moreover, the executor was a stickler for the rules and intended to follow the instructions to the letter.

After a bit of deliberation, Inspector Loo came up with an idea the executor could live with and the heirs could endorse...and that satisfied the demands of the deceased.

What was his plan?

Cash award for the Nobel Prize: 10 million Swedish kronor (about $1.5 million).

61. FLYING FRUITCAKES

There were four finalists in the internationally renowned Fruitcake Toss held every year during the Orange County Apple Festival. As it turns out, the judges lost the results, but luckily, some of the spectators remembered the following snippets of information.

Can you figure out who finished where, and the number and color each contestant wore?

1. The contestants wore the numbers 1 through 4, but only one person wore the same number as the position in which he finished.

2. Gunther, who didn't wear lime green, beat Buddy.

3. Levar beat the person who wore lemon yellow.

4. The person who wore number 3 wore lime green.

5. The person who wore number 2 finished first; Homer came in last.

6. The person who finished second wore lime green, Buddy wore lemon yellow, and the person wearing orange beat the person wearing peach.

By three months of age, babies can recognize facial features.

62. CIRCULAR REASONING

Insert the missing number.

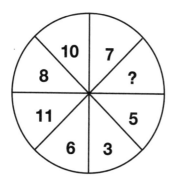

About 80 percent of a dragonfly's brain is devoted to processing visual information.

63. HOMOPHONES

Fill in the blanks in the following sentences with three homophones (words that are spelled differently but sound alike). The dashes indicate the number of letters in the words.

1. My sister is going on a cruise in the Baltic and Caspian _ _ _ _, but first she'll go to a bargain sale at the travel shop and _ _ _ _ _ everything she _ _ _ _.

2. My brother got so upset when he started going _ _ _ _ that he sometimes _ _ _ _ _ _ himself up on the floor and _ _ _ _ _ _ his eyes out.

64. LIGHT MY FIRE

Can you turn FIRE into HEAT in five steps by changing one letter at a time, using common English words each time?

65. LETTER PERFECT

Fill in the blanks to make the sentence true.

In this sentence there are ___ F's, ___ H's, and ___ T's.

66. POSTGRADUATE WORK

Four high school grads have jobs for the summer and are planning to start the same college in the fall, majoring in four different subjects. From the clues, determine each girl's full name, her summer job, and what she has chosen for a major in college.

1. Winona, whose last name isn't Rankin, won't be spending her summer doing office work. Marcia didn't choose Physics for her major.

2. The girl whose last name is Spangler plans to major in Art. Suzanne isn't planning to work as a camp counselor.

3. The girl who chose Education for her major is working as a carhop.

4. Petula, whose last name isn't Culkin, isn't the Education major.

5. The four girls are the girl who's working as a carhop, the girl whose last name is Waring, Petula, and the girl who chose Physics as a major.

6. Suzanne chose French as her major; the girl whose last name is Culkin is working as a barista.

The word "algebra" is from the Arabic *al-jabr*, meaning "restoring."

67. TREACHEROUS TRAVELING

A woman is returning home from Switzerland by train. Luckily, she chose to sit in a smoking car—if she'd been in a nonsmoking car, she'd have died before reaching home. What happened?

68. A GOOD GOOD NIGHT

Can you turn SLEEP into DREAM in six steps by changing one letter at a time, using common English words each time?

69. ABANDONED SHIP

A yacht is discovered in the middle of the ocean. No one is aboard, but several corpses in bathing suits are floating nearby in the water. What happened?

Earliest known robots: Movable statues in ancient Egypt and Greece.

70. FIVE-FLOOR WALK-UP

Andrea, Olivia, Lance, Ivan, and Max live on different floors of an apartment house that's five stories high. Given the following information, can you tell which floor each of them lives on?

1. Andrea doesn't live on the top floor.

2. Olivia doesn't live on the bottom floor.

3. Lance doesn't live on either the top or the bottom floor.

4. Ivan lives on a higher floor than Olivia.

5. Max doesn't live on a floor adjacent to Lance's.

6. Lance doesn't live on a floor adjacent to Olivia's.

71. WHAT'S THE WORD?

Can you think of a word that can be placed in front of each set of five words to form five new words or phrases?

For example, if the words were: CAKE, DOG, FOOT, HEAD, and STUFF, you could add HOT to get HOTCAKE, HOT DOG, HOTFOOT, HOTHEAD, and HOT STUFF. Now you try it:

1. DRAFT, FALL, GRADE, HILL, LOAD, RIGHT

2. AGENT, BOILER, CROSS, DRIBBLE, JEOPARDY, WHAMMY

"Genius is nothing but continued attention." —*Claude A. Helvetius*

72. AT THE MOVIES

The local quadruplex cinema is showing four different movies tonight, including *Grammar School Musical*. Can you match the screen number with the movie being shown and the time each movie starts?

1. *Spaceship to Nowhere* starts either 10 minutes before or 10 minutes after the movie on screen 1 (which doesn't start at 7:00).

2. The movie that starts at 7:30 is showing on either screen 2 or screen 4.

3. The movie that begins at 7:10 is showing at a screen with a higher number than the one that's showing *I Married My Sister's Boyfriend.*

4. The movie that starts at 7:20 is showing on a screen with a number either one higher or one lower than the one showing *Crash Landing* (which starts 10 minutes after the movie showing on screen 3.)

73. SEEK AND FIND

Find the clues and you'll find the message:

T C H L I U S E I C S L A U S E E C C L R U E E T

74. QUITE AN ARRANGEMENT

Can you rearrange the cards according to the following rules?

1. Move as few as possible.

2. Make sure the two columns add up to the same number.

...which had a record 200 competitors in 2006.

75. MAKE MINE A DOUBLE

Joe Java walked into a coffeehouse and ordered a shot of espresso. Instead of firing up the coffeemaker, the barista pulled a gun out from under the counter and pointed it at him. "Thank you," said Joe, as he turned and left.

Why did he thank the barista?

76. ECHOES

What two homophones (words that sound alike but are spelled differently) are being described here?

Underwater lament

77. ABOVE OR BELOW?

The numbers below have been placed according to a particular rule. Can you figure out where to put the 9 and 10?

1	4	7	
2	3	5	6

Christiaan Huygens made the first accurate drawings of Mars in 1659.

78. INSPECTOR LOO AND THE FIRING SQUAD

Guinness-loving gumshoe Inspector Commodius Loo took a day off from crime-solving to play paintball with his buddies. Paintball reminded Loo of his days as an Army Ranger, about which he seldom spoke. And it gave him a way to shoot people without doing any real damage.

Loo and 19 cronies trekked to the paintball range for what had become a ritual boys' day out. It was their habit, at the very end of the game, to mount a faux firing squad, with the guy voted the worst player as the victim. On this unfortunate day, the inspector was it.

The rules gave the shooters one shot apiece. Sometimes a few of them missed, but enough paintballs would typically hit the target to make a big mess of the unfortunate individual.

Inspector Loo, who thrived under pressure, thought fast.

"I have an idea," he told his friends. "Let me choose where you stand when you shoot. I promise not to position you more than 20 feet away, and I'll make sure you're all facing me. I'll bet you a round of beers I can get off without a spatter."

The men were intrigued by this proposal. Where did Loo have them stand?

William Henry Harrison was the only U.S. president with a medical degree.

79. WILD & WOOLLY WORDY

Can you figure out what word or phrase these stand for?

VISION VISION

80. ANAGRAM THIS

An anagram is a word or phrase that's formed by rearranging the letters of another word or phrase. For example, "meat" can be rearranged to get "tame," "mate," or "team." See if you can fill in the blanks below with the two missing words that are anagrams of each other. The number of dashes corresponds to the number of letters in the words.

1. We walked more than a _ _ _ _ to get to the restaurant that served our favorite key _ _ _ _ pie.

2. Jimmy used a special _ _ _ _ to break into the safe and make off with the _ _ _ _.

81. RIDDLER

What kind of animal is it not a good idea to play cards with?

The only humans ever to see the Sun eclipsed by Earth: the crew of *Apollo 12*.

82. WHAT A WAY TO GO

A body is discovered in a big city park in the middle of summer. All of its bones are broken, but an autopsy proves that the cause of death was hypothermia.

What happened?

83. ROPE SWING

Two thin ropes hang from a high ceiling, too far apart to be grabbed with both hands at the same time. How can you tie a knot with both rope ends using only a pair of scissors?

84. SUCCESS STORY

Can you go from POOR to RICH in seven steps, changing one letter at a time, and using common English words each time?

85. I SPY

Three spies were suspected of being double agents. When questioned, here's what they said:

> **Anastasia:** "Boris is the double agent."
> **Boris:** "Natasha is the double agent."
> **Natasha:** "Boris is lying."

Assuming that double agents lie and other agents tell the truth, and there is just one double agent among the three, can you determine who the double agent is? On the other hand, if two of the agents are double agents, who are they?

86. RUSHED TO THE HOSPITAL

One hospital handles all the accident cases in one city, including auto accidents. After the seat-belt law was passed, the frequency of road accidents remained exactly the same, but the hospital became even busier handling the victims of auto accidents. Why?

87. TOM SWIFTY

Tom Swift was the hero in a series of early 20th-century children's adventure books. The author relied heavily on adverbs to describe how Tom was feeling, a style that inspired "Tom Swifties," punny sentences like "'I hate pizza,' Tom said crustily." Below are 10 sentences and 10 adverbs. Use your logical-thinking skills to figure out which sentences and adverbs create the best Tom Swifties.

1. "A thousand thanks, Monsieur," Tom said...

2. "Don't you like my new refrigerator," Tom asked...

3. "I prefer to press my own clothes," Tom said...

4. "I'll have to send the telegram again," Tom said...

5. "I'm burning the candle at both ends," Tom said...

6. "It's the maid's night off," Tom said...

7. "The boat is leaking," Tom said...

8. "The criminals were escorted downstairs," Tom said...

9. "They pulled the wool over my eyes," Tom said...

10. "Welcome to Grant's Tomb," Tom said...

a. balefully	**f.** ironically
b. condescendingly	**g.** mercifully
c. coolly	**h.** remorsefully
d. cryptically	**i.** sheepishly
e. helplessly	**j.** wickedly

...who used his legal knowledge to obtain a full pardon.

88. THE FOUR DOSSIERS

A secret agent is looking at the dossiers of four suspected counterespionage agents (including Rivers), laid out below. From the clues, can you figure out the full name and occupation in each dossier—and identify the double agent?

1. The papers that identify Grimes, who is a missionary, are immediately to the right of Horace's.

2. The dossier at A is Justin's; it doesn't describe him as a polo player.

3. The D dossier does not contain anything about Ralph.

4. One dossier is about Manfred von Troganoff.

5. The business consultant's dossier, which is not next to that of the golf pro, does not give his last name as Edwards; Edwards's dossier isn't in the B position.

6. The polo player's dossier contains proof that he is the double agent.

Actual molecular names: Arsole, bastardane, moronic acid, dogcollarane, and draculin.

89. WILD & WOOLLY WORDY

Can you figure out what word or phrase this stands for?

1, 2, 3...38, 39, LIFE

90. PENGUINS ON PARADE

To save money, five employees of the Aquatic Academy of Science were asked to transport the museum's penguin population to its newly rebuilt exhibit. Can you figure out which car carried which number of penguins—a total of 336 of them?

1. The Hummer carried four times as many penguins as the Volkswagen.

2. The largest group, a third of the penguins, traveled in the Mercedes.

3. The smallest group, 24 penguins, did not go in the Falcon.

4. The Falcon carried 24 fewer penguins than the Civic.

Eighteenth-century astronomer Charles Messier discovered 13 comets.

91. DECISIONS, DECISIONS

Lucille has finally traded in her old jalopy for a spiffy new convertible. Now she has to decide on a color. Eight convertibles are lined up in the car showroom:

The Royal Purple car is at one end, the Snowy White is at the other. The Beet Red car is next to the Midnight Black car and three places to the left of the Sky Blue car. The Sunny Yellow car is next to the Sky Blue car and nearer to the Royal Purple car than to the Snowy White one. The Hi-Ho Silver car is next to the Beet Red one, and the Bottle Green car is five places away from the Sky Blue car. The Midnight Black car is next to the Bottle Green car.

It looks like Lucille is about to choose the fourth car from the left. What color car will she be riding off in today?

92. ONE FOR THE AGES

Jeanine is five times as old as Bobbie. In two years, she'll be three times as old, and in six years, she'll only be twice as old. How old will Jeanine be in seven years?

There are about 300 million neurons in an octopus brain...

93. SOCRATES SPEAKS

Socrates left this secret message for you. Can you figure
out what he was trying to say? (The dashes represent
word breaks.)

AFGTRYT SUGYUJO SDNYTVB MKRRDVB UPMPLKM SVFETVH

ATGTRHJ SEGYURO SDEY–IB MKSRDVB U–OPLNM SVLETYH

HGNDCTY RTUIOMK LMCZSTU WETYUNV OKPLMNH SEFTCVG

–ONDNTY REUI–GK LOCZOTU WDTY–KV ONPLMOH SWFTCLG

FJWBNMK DEVNKOL LPNMSGE KERTYUN SEFTRYV XDCVFRE

FEWBDMK DGVNEOL L–AMSNE KDRT–ON SNFTREV X–EVFVE

SEDCFVG YUOPLKM VBRHTRF CDFRTYU DEVBPKO POUKJHY

SIDCFVG YLOP–IM VBGHTNF COFRTRU DAVBNKO POCKJEY

WERTYFD DFGYHUO BNMKOPX CVBNJUY FRGVBHU VBNJKOP

W–STYFD DOGYCUO BRMKAPX CTBNJEY FRGSBHU VBNJKOP

...and about 100 billion in a human brain.

94. THREE TO FOUR

Move three toothpicks to make four equilateral triangles.
(Note: Nothing may overlap.)

Writing first appeared in China around 1500 BC.

95. ANAGRAM THIS

Rearrange the letters in each entry to make an appropriate corresponding phrase:

> **1.** The earthquake
>
> **2.** Debit card
>
> **3.** The Morse Code

96. AIR TRAFFIC

Barbara's husband called to tell her that he'd just barely made his flight: the 6:35 p.m. Delta flight from San Francisco to Newark. About an hour later, a news bulletin flashed on the movie that Barbara was watching: The 6:35 p.m. Delta flight from San Francisco to Newark had crashed. There were no survivors. Barbara didn't react, just continued to watch the movie. Why?

Scientists have explored just 10 percent of the oceans' depths.

97. OOPS!

A hunter aims his gun carefully and fires. As soon as he does, he realizes that he's made a fatal error. Minutes later, he's dead. What happened?

98. ALL JAZZED UP

The Fab Five All-Girl Jazz Band plays once a week at the Low Down Dirty Saloon, during which each girl does a solo while the band plays the group's favorite jazz songs. From the following statements, what is each musician's favorite song (one is "Lullaby of Broadway")?

1. Martha's least favorites of the five tunes are "In the Mood" and "Autumn Leaves."

2. Neither "It's De-Lovely" nor "When Sunny Gets Blue" is Angelina's favorite.

3. Stella's favorite is one of Martha's least favorites; the other one is Germaine's favorite.

4. Candy's favorite is not "When Sunny Gets Blue."

5. Stella doesn't understand why Germaine doesn't like "In the Mood."

99. THE FIVE NEWSBOYS BY SAM LOYD (1841–1911)

See if you can solve this classic puzzle. Five clever newsboys formed a partnership and disposed of their papers in the following manner:

Tom Smith sold one paper more than one quarter of the whole lot. Billy Jones disposed of one paper more than a quarter of the remainder. Ned Smith sold one paper more than a quarter of what was left, and Charley Jones disposed of one paper more than a quarter of the remainder.

At this stage, the Smith boys had together sold just 100 papers more than the Jones boys had sold. Little Jimmy Jones, the youngest kid in the bunch, now sold all the papers that were left. The three Jones boys sold more papers than the two Smith boys, but how many more?

100. AUTHOR OF THE YEAR

The Author-of-the-Year competition has come down to just four people. In fact, we're about to announce the results. The problem is, the paper the results were written on has disappeared, and the judges can only remember the following facts about the correct order.

Can you figure out the first names, last names, and noms de plume (in quote marks) of the authors, and where they finished in the competition?

1. Chet Fong was not second; he finished one place below Nancy.

2. "Parker Van Dine" finished one place above Tisdale.

3. Neither "Herman Medville" nor "Jeanette Heat" was first.

4. Neither Henry nor Nancy was third.

5. "Mike Wrench," who finished two places in front of "Parker Van Dine," isn't Barry or Pickle.

6. The author whose last name is Austen came in first.

7. The only woman in the group used a woman's name as her nom de plume.

101. SEQUENTIAL THINKING

Can you find the logic behind this series and figure out why it can't be continued?

0, 1, 8, 10, 19, 90

102. TRICKY

At 10 p.m. Shirley turned off the lights in the living room. Her husband, Joe, who had been reading in there, stayed and continued to read for an hour or so. How was this possible? (And no, Shirley and Joe do not live anywhere near the North Pole.)

103. WILD & WOOLLY WORDY

Can you figure out what word or phrase this stands for?

E D O W N
D
I
S

104. NIGHT AT THE ROUND TABLE

Yesterday evening, Winona and her husband invited two other couples to dinner. The six of them sat at a round table. Winona has given you four clues, and she wants to know if you can figure out the name of her husband.

1. Victor sat to the left of the woman who sat on the left of the man who sat on the left of Nicole.

2. Esther sat to the left of the man who sat to the left of the woman who sat to the left of the man who sat to the left of the woman who sat to the left of my husband.

3. Manny sat to the left of the woman who sat on the left of Roger.

4. I did not sit beside my husband.

What is the name of Winona's husband?

105. POOL SHARK

A rectangular billiard table has four pockets, one in each corner. If a ball with unstoppable energy shoots out of one of the pockets at a 45-degree angle to the sides, will it bounce around the table forever or finish up in one of the pockets?

"Patience is a necessary ingredient of genius." —Benjamin Disraeli

106. THE LOGICAL NUMBER

What number should replace the question mark if the fourth set of numbers follows the same logic as the first three?

37, 10, 82
29, 11, 47
96, 15, 87
42, ?, 15

107. WHAT'S THE DEAL?

Let's say you're dealing the cards for a game that requires all the cards to be dealt before the game begins. After about half of the cards have been dealt, the doorbell rings. You put down the undealt cards to answer the door, but when you come back, neither you nor anyone else can remember who got the last card. Without counting the cards in the deck or in anyone's hand, how can you quickly and accurately finish the deal?

108. EVOLUTION

Can you go from APE to MAN in five steps, changing one letter at a time and using common English words each time?

Wine drinkers, on average, have a slightly higher IQ than beer drinkers.

109. YOU DO THE MATH

Take the number of states before Alaska was added. Double that and add the number of seasons. Then subtract the number of Ali Baba's thieves, not counting Ali Baba. Divide by the number of days in the month of February in a leap year plus 1. Cube the result. What do you get?

110. PUZZLE IT OUT

Which two phrases below are closest in meaning?

> **1.** Is the tide turning?
>
> **2.** Are you lost for words?
>
> **3.** Can an early bird get the worm?
>
> **4.** Has the cat got your tongue?

111. ODD MAN OUT

Study the following lists of numbers and identify the one that doesn't belong in each series.

1. 64818, 93618, 54716, 63120, 82313

2. 1623, 9364, 6023, 8421, 6349, 3612, 3062

3. 13, 11, 1255, 273, 5128

4. 4369, 8609, 8162, 6122, 5306

112. SHAPE UP!

The four shapes below each represent a number between 1 and 4. If a circle is worth 3, can you figure out the correct values of the other shapes?

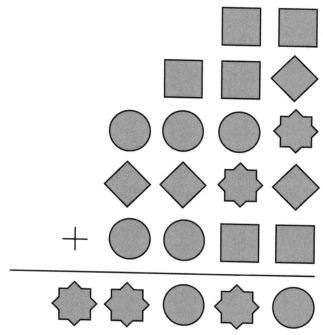

...He won it for his work on the photoelectric effect.

113. CONGA!

For those of you too young to remember, take it from us: Back in the old days, a conga line was the most fun you could have at a party...and the more the merrier. Forming a single line, with your hands on the hips of the person in front of you, you followed wherever the leader went—with a "one-two-three-kick." We decided to revive the lost art form at an office party last week. Can you figure out who took part, and what department each person worked in?

Knowing that fifteen people from three departments took part, every third person worked in sales, and numbers eight and fourteen were editors, can you figure out which of the fifteen worked in the art department, which worked in sales, and which were editors?

1. Helen came after Rickie and Patsy, and before Tori.

2. Cookie came after Donnie and Beau, who came after Gerard, who was before Fantasia.

3. Ollie came before Vern and Patsy, who came before Rickie, who came after Elwood, who came after Patsy, who came after Vern.

4. Darla came after Helen and before Tori, who came before Binky.

5. Gerard came after Zoe, who came after Binky and before Fantasia, who came before Beau, who came before Donnie.

In 1504, Leonardo da Vinci produced wax casts of the ventricles of the human brain.

114. ANAGRAM THIS

An anagram is a word or phrase that's formed by rearranging the letters of another word or phrase. For example, "meat" can be rearranged to get "tame," "mate," or "team." See if you can fill in the blanks below with the two missing words that are anagrams of each other. The number of dashes corresponds to the number of letters in the words.

Poor Richard did not _ _ _ _ _ _ the vision in his right eye after the damage to his _ _ _ _ _ _.

115. WILD & WOOLLY WORDY

Can you figure out what word or phrase this stands for?

VA DERS

116. FOUR SQUARE

Tackle this with the following moves:

1. Move two toothpicks to make seven squares.

2. Remove two toothpicks and leave two squares.

3. Move three toothpicks and leave three squares.

4. Remove three toothpicks and move two to form three squares.

5. Move four toothpicks and form three squares.

6. Remove one toothpick and move four to make eleven squares.

117. NOW THAT'S A CLASSIC

A sailor washes ashore on an island where the inhabitants like to play with strangers before they dispose of them. They offer to let him choose how he wants to be killed. "If you tell a lie," the chief says, "you will be hanged, and if you tell the truth, you will be tickled to death." The sailor can make only one statement. He makes the statement and goes away scot-free.

What did he say?

118. NICE NUMBERS

Each letter stands for a different digit in the math problem below. Can you decode the sum?

```
      T W E L V E
      T W E L V E
      T W E L V E
      T W E L V E
      T W E L V E
      T H I R T Y
     ─────────────
      N I N E T Y
```

...it uses 20 percent of your oxygen supply and 20 percent of your energy.

119. GUILTY OR INNOCENT?

Ellis says, "I'm innocent, Melissa is too." Melissa says, "Kim did it, and Ellis is innocent." Kim says, "I'm innocent, and Melissa did it." If the guilty one lied and the innocents both told the truth, who is the perpetrator?

120. THE THREE TRAVELERS

Here's one of those classic "crossing the river" puzzles: Three travelers, accompanied by their servants, arrive at the bank of a river and want to cross. The only means of transit is a boat that carries two persons. The travelers have reason to believe that the servants have entered into a conspiracy to rob and murder them, should they be able to get the upper hand. So it's essential that a single master should not be left alone with two of the servants, or two masters with all three of the servants. How can the transit be arranged so as to avoid either of the above conditions?

"We are all born ignorant, but one must work hard to remain stupid." —*Ben Franklin*

121. RULES, SCHMULES

There's a common rule for getting the third pattern in each row. Can you figure out the rule and then decide what shape goes in the empty space?

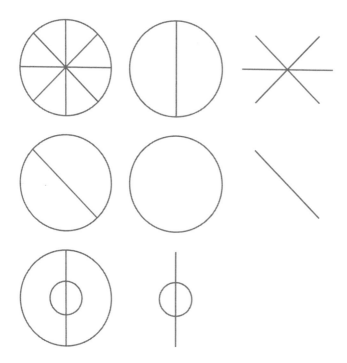

122. NOUVEAU RICH!

Five people in five different California towns just won the lottery, splitting $100 million. On the news, each winner talked about the first thing he or she planned to do with the winnings. From the clues, can you figure out the full name of each winner, what town or city each winner lived in, and what each planned to do with the winnings?

1. Jasper didn't want to take a trip around the world.

2. Ms. Mooney doesn't live in Merced.

3. Miranda didn't plan to build the house of her dreams.

4. The woman whose first move was to quit her job doesn't live in Mariposa.

5. Ariana Sargent wasn't the one who wanted to pay off debts.

6. The person whose last name was Postner wanted to start building a house.

7. Tex's last name wasn't Caruso.

8. Ramona wants to completely redecorate her house.

9. The one who wants to take a trip around the world lives in Salinas.

10. The winner whose last name is Caruso lives in Daly City.

11. Tex's last name isn't Postner.

12. The five winners are the one who lives in Chico, Mr. Peterson, the woman who quit her job, Ariana, and the one who lives in Merced.

123. DON'T PUT THE CART BEFORE THE PONY

Can you go from PONY to CART in only five steps?

124. THE MISSING WORD

NUMBER [BECKON] COOKIE

If you can figure out how the word in the brackets above was created from the first and third words, you should be able to follow the same rules to figure out the word that goes in the brackets below.

RINSED [_____] NOVICE

125. WILD & WOOLLY WORDY

Can you figure out what word or phrase this stands for?

Death   Life

...for being the worst student in his class.

126. CHRISTMAS IN MONEYED MEADOWS

The five wealthy families who live in the gated community known as Moneyed Meadows buy gifts for themselves all year round, but they pull out all the stops at Christmas. Given the clues below, can you figure out which family bought what extravagant gift, and how much each family paid?

1. The Ewings paid twice as much for their gift as the family who purchased the one-month stay at a villa on Capri; the villa wasn't the lowest-priced of the five gifts.

2. The household robot cost its buyers $6,000 more than the Astins paid for their gift; the latter cost $1,000 more than the Andy Warhol drawing that another family bought.

3. The swimming pool for the family dog went for twice the amount of the Carnegies' gift buy—which isn't the Andy Warhol drawing.

4. The Astins didn't buy the month at the villa on Capri.

5. The Forbes family purchase wasn't the household robot.

6. The most expensive of the five Christmas gifts was priced at $20,000; the least expensive sold for $5,000.

7. The gifts included complete nip and tucks for the entire family; the five buyers included the Pirrip family.

127. TEASER

You have a huge pail that, when it's filled to the top with water, weighs 100 pounds. What can you add to the barrel to make it lighter?

128. CUT!

First, imagine this—don't get the scissors just yet. Take a sheet of paper (any size will do). Fold it in half and remember where this first fold is. Then fold it in half again, at a right angle to the first fold. Now you have a four-sheet thickness of paper. Use a pair of scissors to cut the paper right down the middle, perpendicular to the first fold you made. How many pieces of paper do you think you'll have?

129. LANGUAGE EQUATION

If "16 = O in a P" stands for "16 ounces in a pound" what does this equation stand for?

9 = J on the S C

130. MAGIC NINE

Place the numbers 1 through 9 in the hexagons. (Note: Make sure that each side of the triangle adds up to 17.)

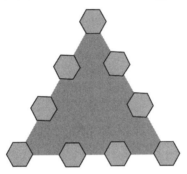

131. A FRIENDLY GET-TOGETHER

Old friends Allison, Ben, Caterina, and Donald meet once a month at the Hill O'Beans Café. Their occupations are—in no particular order—anthropologist, botanist, chemist, and dog walker. At the moment, Donald is telling the botanist that Caterina is going to be a little late, and Allison is sitting across from the dog walker and next to the chemist. The dog walker has just noticed that Ben is starting to lose his hair, but so far hasn't said anything about it. What is each person's occupation?

The game of Chinese checkers was invented in Germany.

132. TIME FOR SCHOOL

Henry had been absent for all but four days in the fall semester. When the principal finally caught up with him, he offered an interesting excuse.

"I don't have time for school. I sleep eight hours a day. That adds up to about 122 days a year. There's no school on Saturday or Sunday, which amounts to 104 days a year. That's 226 days out of the year so far.

"When you add the 60 days of summer vacation, that makes it 286 days. The three hours a day for meals add up to more than 45 days a year. That makes 331 days. You see where I'm going with this?

"And then there's two hours a day for recreation—you gotta give me that—that's more than 30 days a year. You keepin' track? Because that's a grand total of 361 days a year.

"How could I possibly find the time to go to school?"

It took the principal a few minutes to spot the flaw in Henry's reasoning. How long will it take you?

Frederic William Goudy designed 122 different typefaces, including this one.

133. A CLASSIC

Luke had it before. Paul had it behind. Matthew never had it. Girls have it once. Boys can't have it. Mrs. Mulligan had it twice. Mr. Lowell had it once before and twice after.

What is it?

134. THE GANG'S ALL HERE

The police arrested three hapless robbers of a jewelry store when the trio tried to fence their loot. The gang had worn face masks during the commission of the crime, but witnesses came up with enough details for the police to piece together a rough description of each one: name, height, hair color, and which one was the driver, the lookout, and the gunman.

Using the following eyewitness accounts, can you do the same?

1. The gunman was shorter than the lookout.

2. The one called Phil was shorter than the driver.

3. Phil was taller than the bald guy.

4. Lefty was taller than the guy with the blue Mohawk.

5. Junior was shorter than the gray-haired guy.

135. LIES, ALL LIES

If none of the following statements is true, who broke the window?

Mel: Kristen broke the window.

Paul: Mel will tell you who broke the window.

April: Paul, Mel, and I could not have broken the window.

Pat: I did not break the window.

Omar: Mel broke the window, so Paul and April couldn't have.

James: I broke the window, so Paul is innocent.

136. HAPPY COUPLES

Old man Grouchbottom left $100,000 in his will to six beneficiaries: his three sons and their wives. The three wives in total receive $39,600, of which Nell gets $1,000 more than Ursula, and Helena gets $1,000 more than Nell. Of the sons, Mark gets twice as much as his wife, Lonnie gets the same as his wife, and Edwin gets 50 percent more than his wife.

Who is married to whom?

Clinically speaking, death is defined as an absence of brain activity.

137. A NIGHT OUT IN HOLLYWOOD

If Pete Paparazzo doesn't get a picture of hugely popular film star Veronica Hamm tonight, he'll lose his job. He knows she's in one of three nightclubs along Sunset Boulevard, so he tries them one by one. Unfortunately for Pete, there's a bouncer outside each club door who refuses to let anyone of Pete's persuasion in. See if you can help Pete track Veronica down.

- "Where's Veronica Hamm?" he asks the bouncer at club one.

- "Either here or at Club Three," answers the bouncer.

- The Club Two bouncer says, "Club Two or Three."

- The Club Three bouncer is a little more helpful. "She's in Club One or Two, but exactly two of us bouncers are habitual liars."

If only one bouncer is telling the truth, where is Veronica Hamm?

138. WILD & WOOLLY WORDY

Can you figure out what word or phrase this stands for?

ECABT

139. WAY OFF-BROADWAY

The Near-Miss Theatre, which specializes in musicals that would never make it to Broadway, has just announced its upcoming schedule. A different show will be performed on each evening (Tuesday through Friday). Each piece was written by a different composer (including Bernstein), and features a song that you probably won't be humming to yourself as you exit the theater (including "I'm Gonna Wash My Hair Right Offa My Head"). From the information below, can you determine the evening each show will be performed, its composer, and its near-miss showstopping song?

1. The show featuring the song "Ol' Man Swimming Pool" will be performed at some point after *Bye-Bye Birdfood*, but the evening before Sondheim's show.

2. Coward's show (which isn't *Auntie Mamie*) will be performed at some point after the one that culminates with the song "People Will Say We're in Luck."

3. Kern did not write the song titled "Gee, Officer Crumbcake" nor the one called "Surrey with the Flange on Top."

4. "Ol' Man Swimming Pool" isn't from *Fiddler on the Hoof*.

5. *Kiss Me Katz* will be performed at some point before *Fiddler on the Hoof* (which won't be presented on Friday).

Canadian Joseph-Armand Bombardier invented the snowmobile at age 15.

140. GOOD GROOMING

Can you go from COMB to HAIR in seven steps, changing one letter at a time and using common English words each time?

141. THINK ON IT

The center numbers in each of the first two sets were arrived at by applying the same functions to the four numbers around them. Can you figure out what number should replace the question mark in the last set?

21	5	28	13	16	2
24		30		?	
17	7	25	7	10	8

142. PREFERENCES

This word puzzle is all about people who like things that have similarities to the way their own names are spelled. Can you figure it out?

Uncle Marc likes pots and pans but not cooks, straw but not hay, and parts but not wholes. Would he prefer a star or a planet?

Nikola Tesla claimed to have invented a "death ray"...

143. DON'T BE SUCH A WINO

Below are two wineglasses arranged from 10 toothpicks. Can you move six to create a house instead of wineglasses? (Don't overlap or break any.)

...but he couldn't get anyone to invest in it.

144. TRICKY NUMBER 9

Here's a trick that's sure to astound your friends—it even astounds us! All it takes is a calendar that has the dates lined up under the days of the week, so the numbers look something like this:

		1	2	3	4	5
6	7	8	9	10	11	12
13	14	15	16	17	18	19
20	21	22	23	24	25	26
27	28	29	30	31		

Here's what you do: Show someone the calendar and ask him to draw a three-by-three box around any nine numbers on the calendar. Let's say he chooses the bolded nine numbers below:

		1	**2**	**3**	**4**	5
6	7	8	**9**	**10**	**11**	12
13	14	15	**16**	**17**	**18**	19
20	21	22	23	24	25	26
27	28	29	30	31		

Now you're going to tell him—almost immediately—what those nine numbers add up to! Want to know how? Check out the answer section.

145. BROTHERLY LOVE

The Hurley gang consists of three brothers—Earl, Merle, and Burly—who were suspects in three recent robberies. According to the results of the police statements and eyewitness accounts described below, which brothers committed which crimes?

1. Two of the brothers carried out the Hiawatha Casino caper.

2. Two of them broke into the Adorable You Boutique

3. Two of them raided the Blink's armored truck.

4. The one who wasn't in on the Blink's job wasn't involved in the Adorable You Boutique break-in.

5. Burly wasn't at the Adorable You Boutique break-in or the Hiawatha Casino caper.

146. WILD & WOOLLY WORDY

Can you figure out what word or phrase this stands for?

amUous

147. QUICK TRICK

Does the letter I belong with the letters above or below the line?

A H J K
_____
B C D E F G L M N O P Q R S T U V W X Y Z

148. SYBIL'S SIBLINGS

If Sybil has the same number of sisters and brothers, but each of her brothers has only half as many brothers as sisters, how many sisters and brothers are there in the family?

149. UPS AND DOWNS

A nurse worked on the 18th floor of a big metropolitan hospital. When she left her job in the evening, she took the express elevator straight down to the lobby. But when she arrived in the morning, she took the elevator to the eighth floor and walked the rest of the way. It wasn't part of a fitness routine. Why did she choose the stairs?

World's first rockets: The Chinese used bamboo tubes stuffed with gunpowder in 1232.

150. BETTER THAN NONE

The Yreka Bakery makes fresh bread every morning. Let's listen in to this morning's business transactions:

1. Rachel, the first customer: "I'll take half of the bread on the shelf, plus half a loaf."

2. Howie, the second customer: "I'll take half of what you have left, plus half a loaf."

3. Nina, the third customer: "I'll take half of what you have left, plus half a loaf."

4. Marshall, the fourth customer: "I'll take half of what you have left, plus half a loaf."

All four customers left the bakery with what amounted to full loaves. How many loaves of bread did the bakery start with that morning? And how many did each customer take?

151. NOT A NUMBER PUZZLE

What do the following numbers have in common?

3   7   10   11   12   17

The cerebral cortex is about 77 percent of the human brain's total volume.

84

84 84

152. CONNECT THE SQUARES

Without letting your pen or pencil leave the paper, draw six straight lines that connect the 16 squares shown to the right.

The words "oxazepam," "beziques," and "mezquite" can be worth 392 points in Scrabble.

153. INSPECTOR LOO SOLVES THE "LIPSTICK ON HIS COLLAR" CASE

Joe Jones had been murdered on his front porch, his key still in the lock and his wallet missing. Dressed in a business suit, he had apparently been leaving for work when assaulted—or so the police assumed.

But super sleuth Inspector Commodius Loo wasn't so sure. Loo noticed a red lipstick smear on Joe's shirt collar. Surely Jones wouldn't report to the office like that. Loo thought it more likely that Joe was coming in from a night at his girlfriend's when someone shot him.

The cops invited Inspector Loo to interview witnesses. A taxi driver remembered dropping someone off a couple of blocks away. He heard what sounded like a car backfiring around 8:30 a.m.

A woman walking her dog in a nearby park likewise heard a sound, but didn't see anything. Nor did a mailman who had been in the vicinity.

"Poor guy," the mailman said. "Someone must have seen him coming home and attacked him on his porch. But I was in my truck sorting mail—I didn't hear the shot."

Inspector Loo then advised the cops to check with Jones's girlfriend: "If he spent the night at her place, then we have our killer."

Whom did Loo suspect, and why?

The longest Roman aqueduct stretched for 87 miles.

154. FLAMING FLAMINGOS

Every night, some evildoer has been setting fire to the pink plastic flamingos that adorn the front yards along Florida Way. Here's a list of the houses that have been hit:

Monday:	No. 4
Tuesday:	No. 16
Wednesday:	No. 12
Thursday:	No. 3
Friday:	No. 7
Saturday:	No. 28

Do you see a pattern here? Can you figure out where the Flamingo Bandit will strike next?

155. LITTLE GREEN (AND YELLOW AND ORANGE AND PURPLE) MEN

It's the biggest news story in history, and you've been assigned to write it. Just last night, in a field in Nebraska, four extraterrestrials from four different planets arrived within a few hours of each other. The clues below will help you write your big story. Can you figure out the names of the first through fourth to arrive, their colors, the planet each is from, and the number of billions of light-years each traveled to get to Earth?

1. The little green man came from the planet Borkfar, which is 32 billion light years away from Earth.

2. Omina-omina arrived ahead of the ET from Zalkie.

3. The four ETs were Lufgara, the little purple man, the ET from the planet Qiprisca, and an alien who came from a planet that was an even-number of billion light-years away.

4. The little yellow man arrived just ahead of the ET from 16 billion light-years away.

5. The alien who arrived third came from a planet that is 15 billion light-years farther away than that of the little orange man.

6. The alien who arrived immediately after Treb (who didn't arrive first) came from a planet that's 31 billion light-years away.

7. The alien named Wawacha came from the planet Chawawa.

156. WHO'S YOUR DADDY?

Penny Dennington was cruising the aisles at the super-market when she bumped into an old friend she hadn't seen a long time. "What's been happening?" Penny asked.

"Well, I got married in 1999 to somebody you wouldn't know. This is our son," said the friend, who was holding hands with a little boy.

"Hi, little fella. What's your name?" Penny asked.

"It's the same as Daddy's."

"Oh, so it's Jack, huh?"

How did Penny know?

157. WILD & WOOLLY WORDY

Can you figure out what word or phrase this stands for?

CLOUD

TH

A bottlenose dolphin's brain weighs about 100 grams more than a human's.

158. WHAT'S GONE MISSING?

Use logic to find out what goes in the empty square.

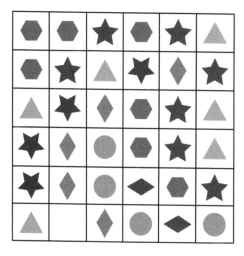

Right-footed African gray parrots have larger vocabularies than left-footed ones.

159. LET'S GET BEAUTIFUL

The New Wave Beauty Salon is in serious need of restocking. There are six employees—three men (Barney, Chuck, and Terence) and three women (Amanda, Chita, and Babs). They ordered a total of nine different items. Four of those items are hair products (hair spray, conditioner, hair clips, and shampoo), and five are body-care products (tweezers, bikini wax, facial masks, nail polish, and massage oil). No two people asked for the same item. From the information, can you figure out the first and last name of each employee and the item or items each one requested?

1. No one requested more than one type of hair product. Amanda isn't the person whose only request was for massage oil.

2. The employee named O'Brien ordered hair spray. One of the women requested both nail polish and hair clips.

3. Terence didn't ask for either conditioner or bikini wax. Three employees who each requested exactly one paper product are Chita, Ms. Parker, and the employee whose last name is Iverson.

4. The employee surnamed Friedman asked for exactly two body-care products. The man who asked for shampoo didn't request any other item.

5. Barney, Terence, and the person surnamed Draper each requested exactly two items.

6. One of the employees is surnamed Feinstein; one of the men's last names is Iverson.

160. LETTER PLAY

Where does the letter T belong? On the top or bottom row?

B D E F H I K L M N P R
A C G J O Q S U V W X Y Z

161. PREFERENCES

This word puzzle is all about people who like things that have similarities to the way their own names are spelled. Can you figure it out?

Aunt Jenny likes ballet slippers but not flip-flops, lemmings but not lemurs, Harry Potter but not Nancy Drew. Following the same reasoning, does she prefer vanilla or chocolate?

On average, the human brain produces about 70,000 thoughts a day.

162. AT THE CROSSROADS

If you were traveling in a strange country without a map and you came to a crossroads where a signpost had been knocked down, how could you find your way without asking anyone for directions?

163. TRANSATLANTIC FLIGHT

You're so rich that you've just bought a private jet. While interviewing pilots, you come across one with a solid résumé. But just to be sure he's the right one for you, you ask him to plot a transatlantic fight to Paris on a flight chart you've brought along. He takes out a ruler and pencil and draws a straight line across the Atlantic.

"Is that the route you'll be taking?" you ask.

"Well, not exactly," he says, "but that would be our planned flight path. Of course, it's mainly computerized navigation and some radio contact nowadays, but it helps to get an idea of visual landmarks, don't you know."

Would you hire him?

The largest known prime number is 9,152,052 digits long.

164. HIGH NOON

A truck broke down at high noon on the main road that runs exactly along the equator in South America. The driver called for help on his cell phone, but knew it would take hours before anyone could reach him.

It was blazing hot: the sun was directly overhead, the telegraph poles that ran parallel with the road weren't even casting a shadow. So the driver crawled under his truck and fell asleep.

When help arrived, the driver emerged and noticed that the telegraph poles now had shadows that seemed to be equal in length to the height of the poles.

Given the fact that the earth rotates at one degree every four minutes, what time was it when help arrived?

165. CHERRY PAIRS

Let's say you had a certain number of pairs of cherries (two cherries whose stems are connected at the top). You gave one friend half your cherries, plus half a pair of cherries. You gave another friend half of what you had left, plus half a pair of cherries. Then gave a third friend half of what you had left, plus half a pair of cherries. Then you had no cherries left.

How many did you start with?

First restaurant to have a robotic staff: Hong Kong's Robot Kitchen.

166. THE CAPTIVES IN THE TOWER BY LEWIS CARROLL

An elderly queen, her daughter, and her little son, weighing 195, 105, and 90 pounds respectively, were kept prisoners at the top of a high tower. The only communication with the ground below was a cord passing over a pulley, with a basket at each end, and so arranged that when one basket rested on the ground the other was opposite the window.

Naturally, if one were more heavily loaded than the other, the heavier would descend; but if the excess on either side was more than 15 pounds, the descent became so rapid as to be dangerous, and from the position of the rope the captives could not check it with their hands. The only thing available to help them in the tower was a cannonball, weighing 75 pounds. They, notwithstanding, contrived to escape. How did they manage it?

167. YOU'VE GOT THE KEY

What is the key to solving this long sequence of curious numbers?

4 23 51   36 26 33 11   5 25   19 20   22 23 9   32 33
51 46 22 24 14 28

168. YAY, TEAM!

There's no crying in baseball—especially among the very successful Bay City Bombers girls baseball team, who depend on four of their players to score most of their runs. Their positions are right fielder, center fielder, left fielder, and shortstop. From the six statements below, determine the girls' first names (Hermione, Cat, Leslie, or Starr), last names (one is Dodson), positions, and batting averages (.280, .295, .310, and .325).

And just to make things more interesting...one of the statements is false.

1. Neither Leslie nor the shortstop has a batting average over .300.

2. Clements, the right fielder, and the player who bats .325 all live on the same block.

3. The center fielder bats .295.

4. Starr's batting average is 30 points higher than that of Cat, who doesn't live near the other three.

5. Brooks and Hermione, who is not Farr, both bat over .300 and are in competition to see who'll score the most runs on the season.

6. Hermione, who is neither the right fielder nor the left fielder, has a lower batting average than the shortstop.

Who was Mary Dixon Kies? The first woman to receive a U.S. patent, in 1809.

169. TOP THIS

Rearrange these nine tops in such a way as to form the greatest number of rows, each row with three tops in a straight line. Eight rows are shown in the picture, but we're sure you can do better than that.

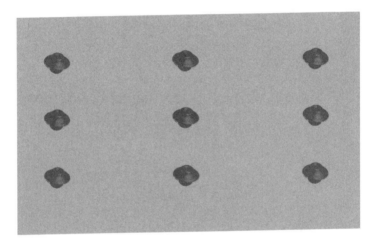

Alexander Graham Bell's favorite bedtime reading material: Encyclopedia Britannica.

170. THE HONEYMOONERS

Five sets of honeymooners at Club Wed spent the day doing a different activity. Each couple brought back a souvenir from their day's adventure. According to the following clues, can you figure out the first and last names of the couples, what they did for the day, and what souvenir they brought back?

1. The couple who went shopping for the day didn't buy the saltwater taffy, but loved what Bart and Deborah bought.

2. Jake, whose last name isn't Marino-Bork, was disappointed by his golfing scores. Thad, who isn't married to Tracy, wanted to go sightseeing with Bart Gallagher-Stein but went surfing with his wife instead.

3. Each of the five couples is uniquely represented by the following: Mr. and Mrs. Harris-Sanchez, saltwater taffy, Cindy, Bart, golfing.

4. Mel is not Tracy's husband and Chloe is not Ed's wife. Ed didn't go hiking.

5. The couple who went sightseeing bought a wind chime; the wind chime and Sarah's model ship were voted the best of the souvenirs.

6. Ed, who isn't married to Cindy, liked the "I Survived Club Wed" T-shirts that Jake Smith-Jones bought. Mel, whose last name is not Helm-Danvers, bought the postcards.

Children's IQs can increase with more schooling and educational toys.

171. SING TO ME

A guy bet his bar mate $100 that he could sing him a song using the name of anyone in the world the bar mate picked. The bar mate thought for a moment and said, "OK, sing me one about Kareem Abdul-Jabbar."

The guy who initiated the bet went home with an extra $100 in his pocket. Which song did he sing?

172. THE FOUR YACHTSMEN

Four wealthy brothers who are avid yachtsmen as well as dog owners have each named a yacht after the dog owned by one of the others. No two yachts have the same name. From the statements that follow, what is the name of each dog (one is Sparky) and each yacht?

> **1.** Bentley's yacht is named after Bobby's dog.
>
> **2.** Buford's dog is named Prince.
>
> **3.** Bradley's yacht is named *Atlas*.
>
> **4.** Buford's yacht is not named *Hercules*.

173. MONEY TALKS

"See," said the gazillionaire to his nephew as he bought another conglomerate. "Money talks." The nephew sighed. "He's right," he said.

"13 15 14 5 25   20 1 12 11 19,   2 21 20 20 15   13 5   9 20   19 1 25 19   7 15 15 4 2 25 5."

Can you figure out what the nephew's last comment is?

174. WILD & WOOLLY WORDY

Can you figure out what word or phrase this stands for?

SYMPHON

175. WHITE HOUSE BOUND

According to the U.S. Constitution, to become president of the United States you have to be at least 35 years old, a citizen, have resided in the United States for at least 14 years, have been born in the United States, and what else?

Sphenopalatine ganglioneuralgia is the scientific name for "brain freeze."

176. THE DISH

If everyone in the village of Melamac owns an even number of dishes, no one owns more than 274 dishes, and no two people own the same number of dishes, what is the maximum number of people in Melamac?

177. WILD & WOOLLY WORDY

Can you figure out what word or phrase these stand for?

CA SE

CASE

178. ANCHOR AWAY

You're sitting in a boat afloat on a lake with no inlet or outlet. You throw the anchor over the side into the water. Does the water level in the pond rise, fall, or stay the same?

179. FOUR DEAD MEN

1. A man was found hanging in an otherwise empty, locked room with a puddle of water under his feet. How did he die?

2. A man was found stabbed to death in a puddle of blood and water on the floor of an otherwise empty, locked room. How did he die?

3. A man was found lying dead in the middle of the desert, with half a match near his outstretched hand. How did he die?

4. Two men in a bar were served identical drinks. One drank his drink quickly and lived; the other took his time and died. What killed him?

Only cats, dogs, monkeys, dolphins, and humans have folds in their brains.

180. TINY BEAUTY QUEENS

Josie and three other little beauty queens entered the Tiny Miss Adorable Cutie-Pie Beauty Pageant. Each wore a different color gown and didn't spill a drop when she had a snack between rounds.

From the clues below, can you figure out who was named Tiny Miss Adorable Cutie-Pie, the order in which the other girls placed, the colors of their gowns, the number that each wore onstage (1 to 4, from left to right), and what snack each ate?

1. The four little girls are Tiffany, the red-gowned one, the one who placed first, and the one who had a hot dog during the break.

2. The tiny miss who came in second stood onstage between the two girls who ate pizza and nachos.

3. Danielle stood next to the little girl who ate a hot dog and the one who came in first in the pageant.

4. The little girl in the green gown had the popcorn and stood two places to the left of Steffi.

5. The girl in the blue gown stood between the red-gowned and yellow-gowned girls.

6. The tiny beauty queen who finished fourth ate pizza.

7. The little miss who ate nachos stood on one of the ends.

The World Scrabble Championship is played on an English-language board.

181. STEP AWAY FROM THAT DESK!

Can you turn WORK into PLAY in nine steps by changing one letter at a time, and using common English words each time?

182. TRICKY

If you lived next door to a peacock farm and one of them flew over to your yard and laid an egg there, would you legally own the egg?

Studies show: Accountants get the most headaches of any profession.

183. WHAT A GLOW!

Can you go from GLOW to WORM in seven steps?

184. THE PRICE POINT

If the prices at your supermarket look like this:

- Steak costs $4.00 per pound.
- An egg costs $2.50.
- A banana costs $4.50.
- Lettuce costs $5.50.

How much would one cucumber cost?

185. QUICK TRICK

Which of the lettered words could logically come next in the following sequence? APE BIRD CAN DIG EAT

a) MAN b) HAT c) CAR d) SEA e) FIG

186. THERE SHE IS...

Charlotte Renfrew invited five girlfriends, including Margo, over to watch this year's Miss America pageant, and each friend brought something yummy to eat. Given the clues below, can you figure out each guest's full name (one last name is Darling), her favorite from among the contestants, and what she brought to eat?

1. Three of the guests were Jenna, the woman whose last name is Martinez, and the Miss Rhode Island fan.

2. The Miss Pennsylvania fan brought quiche.

3. Neither Leslie nor Norma brought the fruit salad.

4. Ms. Martinez wasn't rooting for Miss California or Miss Texas.

5. Ms. Orlando's name isn't Jenna or Kate.

6. The Miss Texas fan didn't bring the deviled eggs or the brownies.

7. Ms. Watson was the Miss New York fan.

8. Neither Jenna nor Kate was rooting for Miss California.

9. Leslie, whose last name isn't Martinez, isn't the one who brought the deviled eggs.

10. Ms. Bronfman didn't bring the brownies.

11. Kate brought paella.

12. Ms. Orlando wasn't rooting for Miss California or Miss Hawaii.

187. GOT CLUE?

Four games of Clue were played over a weekend. In one of them, Miss Scarlett used the candlestick, but not in the library. In another game, the rope was used in the study, but not by Colonel Mustard. During one game, the gun was used in the conservatory.

In another, Professor Plum did it, but not in the library. Colonel Mustard never went near the conservatory, and Mrs. White didn't use the rope to commit her murder. The lead pipe may or may not have been used in the kitchen.

Can you determine who used what and where?

188. WILD & WOOLLY WORDY

Can you figure out what word or phrase these stand for?

Way or weigh

In the third century BC, Egypt's Library of Alexandria contained over 500,000 scrolls.

189. A SQUARE
FULL OF SQUARES

See if you can find another way to use six straight
lines to connect the 16 squares shown below?
(Don't lift your pen or pencil off the paper.)

190. A DAY AT THE DENTIST

Four people, including Mr. Zabriskie, had appointments in the Painless Dentist Building on the same day, but in different rooms and at different times. See if you can figure out the full name of each person, which room their dentist was in, and their appointment time.

1. Abigail's appointment was later in the day than Schmidt's appointment. However, Schmidt's appointment was later in the day than the person in room 103.

2. Mr. or Ms. Nogumi's appointment was at least two hours later in the day than Rocco's appointment.

3. Three of the four dental patients were Deborah, the one with the appointment in room 102, and the person who had an appointment at 5:00 p.m.

4. Mr. or Ms. Jimenez's appointment was later in the day than the person who had an appointment in room 105, who was scheduled later in the day than Carlotta.

191. WORD LADDER

Can you go from HEAD to TAIL in five steps?

The first floppy disk, introduced in 1971, held just 80 KB of data...

192. AN AGE-OLD QUESTION

A man, when asked by his niece how old he was, replied, "My age is now four times yours, but five years ago it was five times yours." How old was he?

193. THE TWO TRIBES

An anthropologist was studying one of those islands where the members of one tribe always tell the truth and the members of the other tribe always lie. She was greeted by two of the islanders—one from each tribe. She asked the taller one, "Are you a truth-teller?"

The islander answered, "Hubba-hubba."

The anthropologist knew this was a native word meaning either yes or no, but she couldn't remember which. The shorter islander spoke English, so the anthropologist asked him what the other fellow had said.

"He said yes," replied the short one, "but he's a liar."

What tribe did each of the islanders belong to?

...Today's Blu-ray DVDs each hold enough data to fill 312,500 old floppies.

194. TEASER

Not counting two dollar bills, what's the most money you can have without being able to change a $20 bill?

195. TRICKY

Answer as quickly as you can: Would you rather be nearly drowned or almost saved?

196. ECHOES

What two homophones (words that sound alike but are spelled differently) are being described here?

Swallowed an octet

Bill for the first transcontinental telephone call: $20.70 for 3 minutes in 1915.

197. DANGER!

When the popular TV quiz show *Danger!* filmed a show recently, host Alec Fourbek quizzed three contestants, including one from Pacific Park, as they vied for cash in the game's three rounds: Danger, Double Danger, and Decisive Danger. At the end of Double Danger, each contestant wagered part or all of his or her winnings on a Decisive Danger question to determine the winner. From the clues below, can you figure out each contestant's full name, hometown, and final score?

1. The three contestants, one of whom is Justin, finished with $17,000 among them; no two had the same amount.

2. During the last round, Barry doubled the money he had won, and Rodriguez added $2,000 in winnings, but the contestant from Forrest Canyon missed the final answer and lost one-third of his or her winnings.

3. The winner, who wasn't Wong, had $3,000 more than the second-place contestant.

4. Canales and the contestant from Santa Teresa both missed the same $2,000 question in the category "Four-Letter Birds" near the end of Double Danger.

5. Amy finished in third place with a total of $4,000.

6. Going into the last round, the three contestants had amassed $13,000 among them.

The right side of the brain understands humor.

198. INSPECTOR LOO NAILS AN INSIDE JOB

It was an inside job. It had to be, graying gumshoe Inspector Commodius Loo muttered as he lit a Pall Mall. Loo had given up smoking years before, but his most recent spate of mysteries had driven him back to it. The distinguished man beside him, curator of the City Art Museum, eyed him sternly. Loo crushed the butt on his boot heel.

It was Sunday afternoon, and the museum's most precious work—a Renaissance masterpiece by Piero della Bagno—had just been stolen. Other than the blank spot where *Madonna and Child* had once hung, there were no clues. The thieves had come and gone during regular museum hours.

Based on the testimony of the security guards, it appeared the picture had disappeared between 10:00 and 11:00 a.m. Loo asked to speak to the four of them.

One claimed he had been patrolling the Egyptian antiquities wing at the time of the heist. The second said he was getting the mail. The third was keeping a child from crayoning a Picasso. And the fourth confessed to sneaking off to a nearby coffee shop.

Loo instantly told the curator who the thieves' accomplice was. Who was it, and how did he know?

Chinese emperors used intelligence testing to evaluate civil servants as early as 2200 BC.

199. MAGIC RULER

A ruler has only four marks on it, but it can still measure the length of any whole number from 1 to 12 inches. One of the marks is 1 inch from the end of the ruler.

Where are the others?

200. YO-HO-HO!

A pirate captain and five of his crew discovered a chest of gold coins. The captain demanded a third of the booty, the first mate wanted a quarter, and the boatswain a fifth. The captain gave the cook an eighth of the loot. Of the remaining coins, he gave 10 to a crewman and one to the cabin boy.

How many coins were there in all?

201. WILD & WOOLLY WORDY

Can you figure out what word or phrase these stand for?
STEP SPETS SPETS

About three soda cans' worth of blood flows through the brain every minute.

202. DADDY DAY CARE

Joe Snowe was a stay-at-home dad and one day ended up taking care of four families of children—including his own.

The Snowe family has the most number of kids, the Bialystocks have a smaller number of children, the Grossingers have a still smaller number, and the Sanchez family is the smallest of all. Altogether, there are fewer than 18 children, and the number of children in each family multiplied together is 120.

How many children were there in each family, and how many did Joe have to take care of that day?

203. SEQUENTIAL THINKING

See if you can figure out what number should replace the question mark in the following series:

19	14	16	32
4	8	2	4
3	3	2	7
5	2	?	4

204. THIS OLD ANTIQUE

Three people visited that popular TV show *This Old Antique* last night, each bringing a family heirloom to be appraised. From the clues, can you figure out which person brought which antique, how much it was worth, and what century each antique was from?

1. The antique brought by Mr. Pointelle was from an earlier century than the Venetian glass vase, which was not worth $1,000.

2. Ms. Bay's antique was worth $600, but wasn't the antique from the 18th century.

3. Mrs. Luce didn't bring the tea set, which fetched the highest appraisal.

4. The serving tray, which was not from the 17th century, was worth more than the Venetian glass vase.

5. The antique from the 19th century wasn't worth $800 and wasn't brought by Mrs. Luce.

205. SMUGGLER

Here's a puzzle that involves a little more than pure logic.
The world's greatest pickpocket has been plying his trade
for more than 20 years all across the globe. He always
brags that he's spent a month in each city before moving
on. If you know he's been seen in the following cities—in
the following order—in the past, can you play detective
and figure out where he'll show up next?

> Seoul
>
> Barcelona
>
> Atlanta
>
> Sydney
>
> Athens
>
> Beijing

206. ECHOES

What two homophones (words that sound alike but are
spelled differently) are being described here?

Steed with laryngitis

207. PLAYING BY THE RULES

Two people are playing a game. Let's listen in.

Player 1 says: A long-necked mammal with reddish-brown blotches.

Player 2 says: A large gray animal with a trunk.

Player 1: A black-and-orange cat found in India.

Player 2: A large mammal with a horn on its nose.

Player 1: A stinky black-and-white mammal.

Player 2: A jumping marsupial from Australia.

Now it's your turn. According to the rules of the game, which of the following should you say?

- A large flightless bird with a long neck.
- A semiaquatic rodent that builds dams.
- A slow-moving reptile with a shell.

208. LET'S GET PERSONAL

Five guests of the Silver Door Spa wanted to spend most of their time with their favorite personal trainers, but there were only four personal trainers available that week. The manager finally came up with a plan that allowed each guest to work out on four of the five days and with the same personal trainer for at least two of the days. Using the clues below, can you figure out the full name of each guest, on which days each guest trained, and which of the four personal trainers they were paired with on those days?

1. Each personal trainer had at least one session with three different women.

2. Bree, who didn't train with Pietro, had the same trainer for three days and a different one on Monday.

3. On Wednesday, the woman whose last name is Winchell trained with George, Ms. Greenberg trained with Pietro, Marcia trained with Ramon, and Dmitri worked with the guest whose last name was Bellini.

4. Pietro worked out twice in a row with both Frieda, who worked with only two of the trainers, and the woman who worked with Dmitri on Friday.

5. Ms. Nelson and Ursula each worked with George on one of the days. Terri worked with three different trainers.

6. On Tuesday, Bree didn't work with a trainer, Ms. Greenberg worked with Dmitri, Maizie worked with the same trainer she worked with for the rest of the week, Ursula Bellini worked with a trainer, and Terri worked with Pietro.

7. Bree, the woman who trained with George on Monday, and Ms. Flaherty all worked with Ramon. Maizie didn't work out on Thursday.

About 30 million neurons in your brain are activated by the sight of a human face.

209. TRICKY, TRICKY

Midway through a transatlantic airmail flight, one bag of mail fell out of the back of the plane. At the very same time, one of the rubber landing wheels fell off the plane, falling vertically. Would the mail bag or the landing wheel hit the ground first?

210. GRADUATION DAY

At the Canine Training Academy, nine dogs stood to attention in a three-by-three square in the following positions. How were the dogs arranged?

> **1.** Max is in the row above Bailey.
> **2.** Molly is in the column to the right of Jake.
> **3.** Rocky is directly to the right of Buster.
> **4.** Phoebe is in the opposite corner to Jake.
> **5.** Flossie is two places to the right of Rosie.
> **6.** Buster is in the column to the left of Max.

211. SUPER SEVEN

Take away one toothpick and move two to leave nothing.

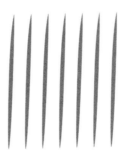

212. POLICE LINEUP

Three petty criminals were in a police lineup, while three eyewitnesses were trying to identify the one they'd seen fleeing a jewelry store right after it had been robbed.

- The first witness said, "Number 1 did it."
- The second said, "It was either Number 1 or 3."
- The third said, "It wasn't Number 1 or Number 2."

If we told you that at least one of the eyewitnesses had been bribed by the culprit and was lying, would you be able to figure out who the perpetrator was?

The Dalai Lama keeps a plastic model of the brain on his desk at home.

213. THE CAT LADIES

Four sisters—Alicia, Bernice, Charlotte, and Denise—have lived together way too long. Each owns two cats, and each has named her cats after two of her sisters. As a result, each lady has two cat namesakes.

- Of the eight cats, three are Siamese, three are Abyssinians, and two are calicos.

- None of the four ladies owns two cats of the same breed.

- No two cats of the same breed have the same name.

- Neither of Alicia's cats is named Denise, and neither of Charlotte's cats is named Alicia.

- No Siamese is named Alicia, and no Abyssinian is named Denise.

- Bernice does not own an Abyssinian.

Given all that information, what are the names of the calicos, and who are their owners?

214. RIDDLER

What do an island and the letter T have in common?

English cop Edward Henry used the first fingerprinting system in 1896.

215. TWELVE SQUARE

Now connect the 12 squares with only five
straight lines without lifting your pen
or pencil off the paper.

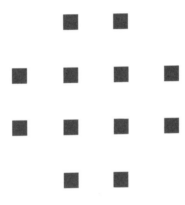

216. WHO OWNS THE ZEBRA?

This classic logic puzzle has been called "Einstein's Puzzle" because it's said to have been invented by Albert Einstein as a boy. Perhaps it was, perhaps not. Either way, in this very slightly edited version, only the cigarette brands have been changed (to cars) to protect the innocent.

1. There are five houses in a row.

2. The Englishman lives in the red house.

3. The Spaniard owns a dog.

4. Coffee is drunk in the green house.

5. The Ukrainian drinks tea.

6. The green house is immediately to the right of the ivory house (as you would face the houses).

7. The Hummer driver raises snails.

8. The Prius belongs to the person in the yellow house.

9. Milk is drunk in the middle house.

10. The Norwegian lives in the first house.

11. The man who drives a Lexus lives in the house next to the man with the fox.

12. The Prius driver lives in a house next to the house where the horse is kept.

13. The Mercedes driver drinks orange juice.

14. The Japanese man drives a Cadillac.

15. The Norwegian lives next to the blue house.

Now, who drinks water? And who owns the zebra?

Harvard's Brain Tissue Resource Center has some 3,000 donated human brain specimens.

217. THE AMAZING NUMBER 73

Write "73" on a piece of paper, fold it up, and give to an unsuspecting victim...er, person. Tell her she's not to look at it until you say so. Next, ask her to think of a four-digit number and enter it twice into a calculator, for example: 36,243,624.

Tell her to divide the number by 137, then divide that result by the original four-digit number. After she's done it, tell her to open the piece of paper you gave her earlier. It will match the display on the calculator. That's right— the amazing number 73!

Want to know how it works? Check out the answer section.

218. WORD GAME

There are lots of English words that become plural when you add an S at the end. There are also a few that become singular again if you add another S—like CARE, CARES, and CARESS. We've thought of two more that fit the category.

How many can you think of?

Ancient Egyptians believed that the brain was just stuffing...

219. I'LL HAVE WHAT HE'S HAVING

A guy walks into a bar and asks for a beer. "Do you want the regular beer for $2.90 or the special beer at $3?" asks the bartender. "I'll take the special," says the man. Shortly after that, a second man walks into the bar, places $3 on the counter, and says, "Gimme a beer, please." The barman glances at the money and pours him the special beer. Given that both customers had never been to the bar before, can you think of a reason that the bartender would be so sure what the second customer wanted?

220. PREFERENCES

This word puzzle is all about people who like things that have similarities to the way their own names are spelled. Can you figure it out?

Aunt Barbara likes bagels but not English muffins, topaz but not opal, jargon but not lingo. Would she prefer Cancun or Puerta Vallarta?

221. MAGIC NUMBER SIX

Can you figure out how to use three 6s to make a 7?

222. LANGUAGE EQUATION

If "16 = O in a P stands for 16 ounces in a pound," what does this equation stand for?

$$52 = C \text{ in a } D$$

223. QUICK TRICK

Why is more toilet paper purchased in the United States than Canada?

224. WILD & WOOLLY WORDY

Can you figure out what word or phrase these stand for?

m ce
m ce
m ce

In 1991, Hungary Judit Polgar became the youngest chess grand master, at age 15.

225. HOURGLASS FIGURES

You've got a 7-minute hourglass and an 11-minute hourglass. What's the quickest way to time the boiling of some pasta for 15 minutes?

226. TO YOUR HEALTH!

Three men have given up driving to work in favor of healthier ways of commuting. From the clues below, can you figure out each one's full name (including Mr. Portnoy's), where each one works (including Acme Transport), and how each one now gets to work (including taking the bus)?

1. Neither Jerry nor Mr. Weller rides a bike to work.

2. Stu, who works at the Fizzy Cola bottling plant, is not Mr. Hurley.

3. Christopher, who doesn't work at Pierre's French Laundry, jogs to work.

There are about 3 million miles of axons in the human brain.

227. QUICK TRICK

In which direction does the Danube flow?

228. THE COPS GET THEIR MAN

Acting on an anonymous phone call, the police raid a house to arrest a suspected murderer. They don't have a description—all they have to go on is that his name is Perry and he's inside a particular room. They break in on a butcher, a plumber, a ditchdigger, and a firefighter all playing poker. Without hesitation or communication of any kind, they immediately arrest the plumber.

How do they know they've got the right man?

229. ECHOES

What two homophones (words that sound alike but are spelled differently) are being described here?

Forbidden music group

230. THE ENGINE DRIVER BY BORIS KORDEMSKY (1900)

Try to solve this classic puzzle: On the Moscow–Leningrad train are three passengers named Ivanov, Petrov, and Sidorov. By coincidence, the engine driver, the fireman, and the guard have the same three last names.

1. Passenger Ivanov lives in Moscow.

2. The guard lives halfway between Moscow and Leningrad.

3. The passenger with the same name as the guard lives in Leningrad.

4. The passenger who lives nearest the guard earns exactly three times as much per month as the guard.

5. Passenger Petrov earns 200 rubles a month.

6. Sidorov (a member of the crew) recently beat the fireman at billiards.

What is the engine driver's last name?

231. TRIXIE'S KIDS

The last census taker who'd knocked on Trixie Lott's front door had gone away shaking his head and retired from the business soon after. This time around, though, the census taker was also a lover of puzzles.

First, he asked Trixie how many children she had and got the reply "Three." But when he asked for their ages, Trixie refused to say. "I'll give you a hint," she said. "If you multiply their three ages, you get 36. And, by the way, their ages are all whole numbers." The census taker thought for a moment, then asked for another hint. So Trixie said, "The sum of their ages is the number on the house next door." After checking the number, the census taker asked for one final hint. When Trixie answered, "Tomorrow is my oldest child's birthday," the census taker jotted down a few numbers and came up with the right answer.

What are the ages of Trixie's three children?

232. STICK IT

In this puzzle, move one stick to make a square.

233. CASINO NIGHT

Five lucky people at Las Vegas High School's annual Casino Night are waiting in line to collect their winnings. From the following information, can you figure out who is first in line, the order of the other four behind him or her, the game each was playing, and the amount of cash each collected?

1. The fourth person in the line was playing poker; Bernadette, who won $20, is ahead of him or her.

2. The third person in the line will collect the smallest amount; the blackjack player won the highest amount.

3. The amount won at the roulette table was greater than the amount that Carrie won.

4. Olivia won her money playing craps.

5. Freddie is immediately ahead of Maribelle in the line.

6. Both the person at the head of the line and the winner at bingo are women, and both are collecting less than Freddie.

7. The amounts of money being collected are $10, $20, $30, $40, and $50.

Eddie Van Halen, Michael Jackson, and Harry Connick Jr. all hold U.S. patents.

234. LANGUAGE EQUATION

If "16 = O in a P stands for 16 ounces in a pound," what does this equation stand for?

1,001 A N

235. PUZZLING PEOPLE

Four puzzle aficionados have cooked up a challenge for you. Of the five statements below, only one is true. Can you figure out which person prefers each kind of puzzle?

(And don't forget: only one statement is true, and the others are false.)

1. Jillian prefers either math puzzles or crosswords, and Jeff loves matchstick puzzles.

2. Either Camilla or Charles prefers word-search puzzles.

3. The matchstick puzzle person is Charles, Jeff, or Jillian.

4. Either Charles or Jillian prefers word-search puzzles; the other prefers math puzzles.

5. Camilla likes either crosswords or math puzzles.

236. QUICK TRICK

Can you figure out the values of X and Y ?

7 8 6 9 5 10 X Y 3 12

237. SUPERHEROES

Jordan Green, Morgan Black, and Cameron Blue attended a come-as-your-favorite-superhero party. They came dressed as the Green Lantern, Black Lightning, and the Blue Devil.

At one point, Jordan said to the partygoer dressed as Black Lightning, "Did you notice that the three of us are dressed as superheroes whose names don't correspond to our real names?"

Who wore what to the party?

238. ECHOES

What two homophones (words that sound alike but are spelled differently) are being described here?

Strange open market

239. GOT LOOT?

A man was digging a garden and unearthed a large chest that was filled with money and jewels. He didn't spend any of the money, nor did he tell anyone what he'd found until four years later, when he suddenly bought a new house, a new car, and a whole new wardrobe. Why?

240. WORD LADDER

Can you go from DEAD to LIVE in six steps?

241. THE NIGHT SHIFT

The night watchman at a factory went to work after eating a heavy meal. The next morning, he told his boss about a dream he'd had: Someone was planning to sabotage the factory. The watchman thought it was a warning. After listening to the story, the boss promptly fired him. Why?

Alexander Graham Bell invented a device for locating icebergs.

242. AT HOME WITH THE WELLOFFS

The Welloffs are just like any other couple, except they're rich and, along with three of their servants, star in the hit TV reality program *At Home with the Welloffs*. The show airs Monday through Friday, and each episode features a different member of the household. From the clues, you should be able to figure out this week's schedule, which household member stars in each show, and what he or she did to cause that night's pandemonium.

1. One show features the Welloffs' cook Kristina; another revolves around a household member who gets locked in the meat freezer and emerges covered in dangling icicles.

2. The episode starring Mrs. Welloff is on the evening before the show where one household member helps a neighbor move a piano.

3. The program centering around one household member's run-in with a used-car salesman is on the night before the show featuring Bob the chauffeur.

4. The evening before Mr. Welloff is featured, one household member decides to join a karaoke club.

5. The episode during which one member of the household holds a séance is on the day before the show that features Jessica the maid.

6. Bob, who isn't the center of Tuesday's show, isn't the one who helps move the piano.

7. Mr. Welloff isn't the one who has the run-in with the used-car salesman.

8. The household member who joins the karaoke club isn't Mrs. Welloff.

IQ scores have risen approximately 20 points with every generation tested.

243. LETTER PERFECT

Fill in the blanks to make the sentence true.

In this sentence there are ___ R's, ___ T's, ___ two V's.

244. ECHOES

What two homophones (words that sound alike but are spelled differently) are being described here?

Spots locations

245. WHAT DO YOU THINK?

Don't write anything down or use a calculator. Use logic to figure this one out: Are there more 2s or 8s to be found in all the numbers from 1 to 50,000?

246. CAREFUL WHAT YOU WISH FOR...

Jim Judd bought an unusual brass lamp at an antiques shop. When he got it home and began polishing it, out popped a genie. As genies will, this one promised him a single wish and gave him a day to ponder it.

Jim discussed the matter with his wife, who urged him to ask for a daughter. They already had three boys, and she dearly wanted a girl. Then he went to see his father, who was blind. His dad asked Jim to wish for his eyesight back.

Jim himself wanted a lot of money, so he could adequately care for both his aging father and his many offspring, ensuring an Ivy League education for the latter.

What did he wish for that satisfied all their desires?

...20 years before the technology existed to prove it.

247. AT THE STORE

The aisles in Marv's Mini-Mart are numbered one to six, starting at the entrance.

- Cleaning products are in the aisle next to beverages, and aren't the first items you see when entering.
- The meat aisle is closer to the entrance than the bread aisle.
- Cereals are two aisles before beverages, and meat is four aisles after produce.

How are the aisles arranged?

248. NOT YOUR GRANDDAD'S CRYPTOGRAM

This may look like a normal cryptogram, but there's something different about it. The encrypted message will tell you what the secret of the code is. Can you solve it? (Hint: It's not as difficult as it looks.)

UJH GKUWY MGWXJX JU BFYESILL CA PPH

QQVMYOVV, UJH TGFSSJ MGWXJ CA UYR

QQVMYOVVB, BPG TQ PP...

A poem written in 270 BC lists 48 constellations...

249. SIBLING RIVALRY

If Buddy had one more sister, he would have twice as many sisters as brothers. If he had one more brother, he would have the same number of sisters and brothers.

How many brothers and sisters does Buddy have?

250. MOMMY'S LITTLE GIRL

If a mother is four times as old as her daughter, and in 20 years will be twice as old as her daughter, how old are mother and daughter now

251. CAPITAL PUN-ISHMENT

The clues below are puns on particular words or phrases. The numbers in parentheses give you a hint; they refer to the number of letters in the answer, for example "helping hand" would be (7,4).

Pot of ale (4, 5)

252. THE THREE SISTERS

Dorothy, Christine, and Phyllis are all under 21 years of age. Dorothy is now as old as Phyllis was 14 years ago, and two-thirds of Christine's age. Christine, on the other hand, will be Phyllis's age when Christine is twice as old as she is now plus two years. Three years ago, Christine was as old as Dorothy is now.

How old are Dorothy, Christine, and Phyllis now?

253. LANGUAGE EQUATION

If "16 = O in a P stands for 16 ounces in a pound," what does this equation stand for?

26 = L in the A

254. TURN THAT FROWN UPSIDE DOWN

Can you turn TEARS into SMILE in six steps?

Scotsman John Napier published the first tables of logarithms in 1614.

255. ANAGRAM THIS

Rearrange the letters in each entry to make an appropriate corresponding phrase:

> **1.** The eyes
>
> **2.** Election results

256. PICK A NUMBER, ANY NUMBER

Ask someone to pick a number between 1 and 9. Now, with a calculator, have him first multiply the number by 9, then by 12,345,679 (that's the numbers 1 through 9 with no 8). Now ask the person to show you the result. If the answer on the calculator is 555,555,555, the number the person selected was a 5. If he selected 3, the answer is 333,333,333. Want to know how it works? Check out the answer section.

257. TEASER

How many animals of each sex did Moses take on the ark?

More than 1 million U.S. patents have been granted in the last five years alone.

258. THE CHECK'S IN THE MAIL

Can you go from BLANK to CHECK in five steps, changing one letter at a time and using common English words each time?

259. IT'S A BARGAIN

You've spent the last year building your home. Now it's time to add an important part to your project. When you go to the hardware store to get what you need, the items are priced as follows:

- One will cost $5.
- Two will cost $5.
- Twelve will cost $10.
- A hundred and forty-four will cost $15.

What are these items?

260. QUICK TRICK

Is there any way you can prove that 7 is half of 12? Feel free to be tricky.

261. WHISTLESTOP WHEELS

The Whistlestop Wheels van picked up five passengers at Morris Avenue, four of whom got off the van at each of its next four stops, from First through Fourth streets. The fifth passenger rode the bus all the way to the end of the line. As each original passenger got off at First to Fourth streets, one new passenger got on and rode all the way to the end, where all five passengers got off. Given the statements below, can you figure out the full names (one first name is Edith and one last name is Costa) of all the Whistlestop Wheels passengers, who got off and on at each stop, and who rode all the way from Morris Avenue to the end? (Note: In the clues, "got on" and "got off" mean at First to Fourth Streets only, not the ends of the bus route.)

1. As Hilda got off the van at one stop (not Third Street) Orwell got on.

2. John and Robertson ride the van every day.

3. Vincent got off the van at a later stop than where Westwood got off.

4. As the bus slowed to a stop at Third Street, the five passengers on board were Bernice, Xavier, Robertson, Ulrich, and Vanderbeer.

5. Yolanda French got off the van one street after Merkowitz got on.

6. Xavier's last name isn't Orwell.

7. Frances was riding the van when it arrived at the very last stop.

8. Bernice, Orwell, and Merkowitz all buy monthly passes for unlimited Whistlestop Wheels service.

9. Honey Graham got on the van one street after John got on.

10. Vincent's last name is neither Robertson nor Vanderbeer.

262. BEST IN SHOW

The Eastminster Poodle Hybrid Show has just concluded, but you arrived too late. You'll have to use the clues below to figure out who handled which dog, what class each competed in, how each dog placed, and the breed of each dog.

1. If Woof finished first, then Terence's dog finished fourth.

2. If Terence's dog finished fourth, then Ruff is a Cockapoo; otherwise, Ruff is not a Cockapoo.

3. If June's dog competed in the Senior class, she finished third; if she competed in Novice, she finished fourth.

4. The dog that finished ninth was a Yorkipoo. This was either Ruff, in which case Ruff competed in the Open class, or this was Yip-yip, in which case Terence handled Yip-yip.

5. Bill's dog won in the Puppy class.

6. If Bill's dog is Arfur, then Arfur is a Labradoodle; otherwise, Arfur is a Cockapoo.

7. Ruff is Ruth's dog.

8. If Ruff finished fourth, she competed in the Novice class; otherwise, she competed in the Senior class.

9. If Arfur finished first, Terence's dog is a Yorkipoo; otherwise, Terence's dog is a Cockapoo.

10. If June's dog is a Giant Schnoodle, June finished fourth; otherwise, June finished third.

Marie Curie's daughter Irène won a Nobel Prize for chemistry in 1935.

263. IT'S A LIVING

Alfie, Buford, Cedric, and Raymond are an architect, a barber, a caseworker, and a dentist, but not necessarily in that order. Given the following facts, can you determine what each man's occupation is?

1. At least one, but not all, of the men's names begin with the same first letter as their occupations.

2. The architect's name does not contain an "r".

3. The barber and dentist each have names that share exactly two letters.

"If the facts don't fit the theory, change the facts." —*Albert Einstein*

264. PLAYING CARDS

There are three playing cards lying faceup, side by side. A four is just to the right of a three. A four is just to the left of a three. A diamond is just to the left of a heart, and a diamond is just to the right of a diamond. What are the three cards?

265. WILD & WOOLLY WORDY

Can you figure out what word or phrase these stand for?

MACBETH

WORDS

266. ECHOES

What two homophones (words that sound alike but are spelled differently) are being described here?

Underage prospector

267. THE MARRYING KIND

The aging but still glamorous movie star Elizabeth Garland has always had a weakness for younger men—she's married a grand total of five of them. From the clues below, can you figure out the name and age of each of Liz's husbands at the time of their marriage, and where they were married?

1. The young man Liz married in Los Angeles was older than both her immediately previous groom and Donald, whom she married in 2000.

2. Stan was 20 when he and Liz were married; this was not the 1996 wedding.

3. Marco, the fellow Liz wed in Venice, was older at the time of their marriage than Abel, who was not Liz's first husband.

4. The 19-year-old groom didn't marry Liz in London.

5. The husband Liz married in 1985 was 18 at the time.

6. The marriage to the 22-year-old took place earlier than the one in New York, but was not the immediately preceding ceremony.

7. The Beijing wedding took place sometime before the one in which Liz wed Jorge, who was a younger groom. Liz's wedding to the oldest of the five (who was 23 at the time) didn't take place in 1978 or 1991.

Only 5 percent of American neurosurgeons are female.

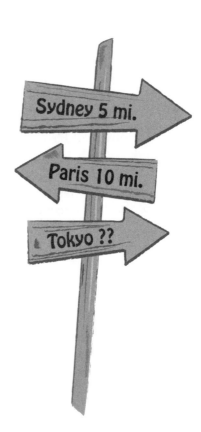

268. THE SIGN SAYS?

By following the same rules used for this sign, how far is it to Tokyo?

269. BLACK HATS VS. WHITE HATS

In this classic puzzle, a professor gathers four students into a circle around him and shows them seven hats: four black and three white. He blindfolds them and puts a hat on each of their heads. When he removes the blindfolds, he asks each in turn if he or she can tell him the color of the hat they're wearing, and if they answer, they'd better be sure.

- The first student says, "I don't know."
- The second student says, "I don't know either."
- The third student says, "Nor do I."
- The fourth student says, "My hat is black."

How did the fourth student know the color of her hat?

270. FERTILE FIELDS

Can you go from WHEAT to BREAD in seven steps, changing one letter at a time and using common English words each time?

...recognize up to 10 different human faces and address each by name.

271. NUMBER PROBLEM

What mathematical symbol can you put between 3 and 7 to get a number bigger than 3 and smaller than 7?

272. YES DICE

A six-sided die has three sides that say "YES"; the other three sides say "NO." What one question about the outcome will the die answer truthfully, no matter what the result of the roll is?

273. WILD & WOOLLY WORDY

Can you figure out what word or phrase these stand for?

H I J K L M N O

Over a lifetime, college graduates earn $812,000 more than high school dropouts.

274. TEASERS

1. Felicity had two pairs of twins twice. How many children does this make?

2. If a book has 100 leaves—pieces of paper that contain pages on each side—on what leaf would page 49 be?

275. TRIANGULATE THIS

Make four equilateral triangles from these six toothpicks without breaking any.

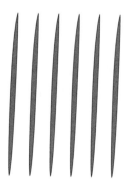

Your brain is full of nerve cells, but it has no pain receptors.

276. FIGURE IT OUT

You've got two empty jugs: a three-gallon jug and a five-gallon jug. How can you measure exactly one gallon?

277. QUICK TRICK

Which number in the following series is least like the others?

1   3   5   7   11   13   15

278. SCAPEGOAT

Can you go from SHIFT to BLAME in eight steps, changing one letter at a time and using common English words each time?

279. ROBBERY ON THE ORIENT EXPRESS

When notorious international criminal Roberto de Starz robbed the Orient Express, he took a total of $25,000 from four of the passengers. Each of the four victims, including Princess Ann of Monglovia, lost a different sum to the infamous thief. From the conductor's report below, can you figure out where on the train de Starz held up each person (one was robbed while sitting in the passenger coach), and how much money did he steal from him or her?

1. Immediately after robbing Doctor Humphrey Fahrquar of his whole bankroll, de Starz held up another of the victims in the sleeper car—for $2,500 more than he got from the doctor.

2. Friedrich Von Monocle did not lose the most money of the four.

3. Immediately after robbing the victim who was trying to hide behind a barrel in the baggage car, de Starz took Madame Sheeza Tutzibelle's cash, $7,500 less than he stole from the victim in the baggage car.

4. The person de Starz held up in the dining car didn't lose the smallest sum, $2,500, to the villain of our piece.

280. SMOOCHY STRIKES AGAIN

Can you turn KISS into LOVE in five steps by changing one letter at a time, using common English words each time?

281. AND THE NUMBER IS?

What number finishes this series?

1   2   3   7   22   ?

    a. 52

    b. 68

    c. 126

    d. 154

    e. 155

282. LONG LIVE THE EMPEROR!

The famous Roman emperor Sillius Maximus was born on January 1, 40 BC, and died on January 1, AD 40. How old was he when he died?

Cost of a one-year subscription to the journal *Brain Research*: $22,386.

283. SEQUENTIAL THINKING

See if you can figure out what number should replace the question mark in the following series:

9, 16, 25, 36, ?

284. ON YOUR MARK...

The results of an intramural race were as follows: The student who came in two places behind the winner also came in three places above the student who came in last.

How many students races?

285. WONDERFUL WORDPLAY

Find the two words that are most nearly opposite in meaning:

Intense
Extensive
Majority
Extreme
Diffuse

The left hemisphere of the brain has 186 million more neurons than the right.

286. THE "IGOTCHA" DIAMOND

All the eligible young men in the kingdom of Igotcha wanted to marry Princess Brainia, so her father the king set up a series of puzzles for them to solve. In this one, there are three boxes bearing three inscriptions. Keeping in mind that at least one inscription is true and at least one is false, can you tell which box contains the 84-carat Igotcha Diamond for the princess's engagement ring?

Gold box: The diamond is not in the silver box.

Silver box: The diamond is not in this box.

Titanium box: The diamond is in this box.

Q: What do Geena Davis, Jodie Foster, and porn star Asia Carrera have in common?

287. RIDDLE ME THIS

1. Read forward, I am heavy. Read backward, I am not. What am I?

2. Which girl's name does this make you think of? *I*

3. What's the tallest kind of building in the world?

288. HAIR TODAY, A CLASSIC

You find yourself in a strange town, badly in need of a haircut. There are two barbers in town, each with his own shop. The first shop you see is extremely dirty; the barber needs a shave, his clothes are messy, and his hair is unkempt and badly cut. The second shop is clean as a whistle; the barber is clean-shaven, dressed neatly, and his hair is perfectly trimmed. Which shop would you go to and why?

289. WILD & WOOLLY WORDY

Can you figure out what word or phrase these stand for?

THEAWALKPARK

290. CIRCLES SQUARED

Puzzle #1. How many perfect squares (all sizes are OK) are hidden in the cross of circles below? (Note: A square counts if any four circles are placed in its corners.)

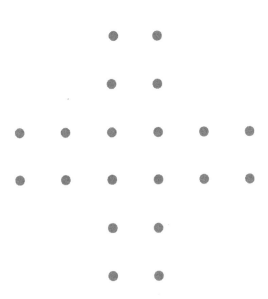

Puzzle #2. This one's harder. Remove six circles so that any four circles left won't lie in the corners of a square and so that no four circles form a perfect square.

291. DIGITS

What three-digit number is described by these clues?

My tens digit is five more than my ones digit.

My hundreds digit is eight less than my tens digit.

292. TEASER

Two old men just finished playing five games of checkers. Each man won the same number of games, and there were no ties. How can you explain this?

293. WONDERFUL WORDPLAY

Here's an extra-tricky question: Can you make a word from "boas" that can be used to keep you clean?

294. QUICK TRICK

A coin is inside a corked bottle. How could you extract the coin from the bottle without breaking anything or removing the cork from the bottle?

295. AND THE NUMBER IS?

What number should replace the question mark?

13   44   88   176   847   ?

296. IT WAS HERE A MINUTE AGO...

Can you turn LOST into FIND in five steps by changing one letter at a time, and using common English words each time?

297. ECHOES

What two homophones (words that sound alike but are spelled differently) are being described here?

Bed in a maternity ward

298. ONE BIG HAPPY FAMILY

In a photo taken at a family reunion were one grandfather, one grandmother, two fathers, two mothers, four children, three grandchildren, one brother, two sisters, two sons, two daughters, one father-in-law, one mother-in-law, and one daughter-in-law.

If we told you there were not as many people as our list makes it sound, can you tell how many people were in the photo?

299. ROOM FOR IMPROVEMENT

Can you go from FAIL to PASS in only four steps, changing one letter at a time, and using common English words each time?

Swordfish have a special tissue behind their eyes that raises their brain temperature.

300. A MOTHER'S LOVE

Once upon a time, in a faraway land, there lived a queen named Bubbles and her beautiful daughter Princess Porcelain. The princess wanted to get married, but Queen Bubbles wouldn't allow it. (She never wanted Porcelain to leave the throne room.)

So Bubbles came up with a plan to rid the palace of suitors. All a suitor had to do to win Porcelain's hand was to draw a piece of paper from a golden bowl. But there was a catch: There were two pieces of paper in the bowl. One said "My Child," resulting in marriage to the princess. The other said "The Snakes," which meant the suitor would be thrown into a pit of poisonous snake...never to be seen again. Somehow the suitors always chose the piece of paper that sent them to the snake pit.

One day, a handsome knight named Sir Flushalot came along and Porcelain fell head-over-heels for him. the princess pulled him aside and whispered, "I think my mother is a cheat. I believe both pieces of paper say 'The Snakes.'" Flushalot assessed the situation and said, "Fear not, beautiful lady. I have a plan."

Aware that he couldn't expose the queen as a cheater, how did Flushalot win Princess Porcelain's hand in marriage?

Of oxygen consumed by the brain, 6 percent will be used by the brain's white matter...

301. SEQUENTIAL THINKING

See if you can figure out what number should replace the question mark in the following series:

$$5 \quad 9 \quad 17$$
$$13 \quad 25 \quad 49$$
$$37 \quad 73 \quad ?$$

302. FACE TIME

Inspector Commodius Loo bought two clocks from Gordo's Repair Shop and set them at the same time. He soon discovered, though, that one clock was two minutes slow per hour and the other was one minute fast per hour. The next time the inspector looked, one clock was exactly an hour ahead of the other. how long had it been since he last set the clocks?

303. ECHOES

What two homophones (words that sound alike but are spelled differently) are being described here?

Precious buck

304. TRICKY

If Teddy Roosevelt were alive today, what would he be most noted for?

305. FLYING HIGH

Consider this: You're sitting on a bus. The kid next to you has a helium-filled balloon and it ends up against the ceiling, just about in the center of the bus. The driver suddenly hits the breaks, and the bus lurches forward, throwing you back into your seat. What does the balloon do?

306. WHEN IN ROME...

Which letter comes next in this series? The answer is neither I nor X.

I X X X I X I I I I I I I I I ...

307. HOMOPHONE

Fill in the blanks in the following sentence with three homophones (words that are spelled differently but sound alike). Dashes indicate the number of letters in the words.

I was so poor that it didn't make any _ _ _ _ _ to spend 99 _ _ _ _ _ on the _ _ _ _ _ _ at the perfume shop.

308. NOBODY'S FOOL

Can you go from FOOL to SAGE in six steps?

309. CAPITAL PUN-ISHMENT

The clues below are puns on particular words or phrases. The numbers in parentheses give you a hint—they refer to the number of letters in the answer; for example, "helping hand" would be (7,4).

Charge of the light brigade (8, 4)

...So the company renamed it "BHA"—for "Butthead Astronomer."

310. WILD & WOOLLY WORDY

Can you figure out what word or phrase this stands for?

O_ER_T_O_

311. RUSHED TO THE HOSPITAL

One hospital handles all the accident cases in one city, including auto accidents. After the seat-belt law was passed, the frequency of road accidents remained exactly the same, but the hospital became even busier handling the victims of auto accidents. Why?

312. ECHOES

What two homophones (words that sound alike but are spelled differently) are being described here?

Light-colored bucket

313. GRIDDY NUMBERS

Can you put the numbers 1 through 8 in the following grid so that no consecutive numbers touch vertically, horizontally, or diagonally?

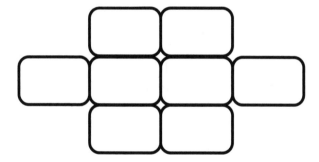

Children are considered gifted if their IQ is higher than 130.

314. INSPECTOR LOO SNIFFS OUT AN ANSWER

Inspector Commodius Loo was downtown getting his gun repaired when he noticed police cruisers at world-renowned jeweler Manicotti's. Sgt. Hal Smith told Loo that a couple of thugs had just robbed the place in broad daylight.

"We've got witnesses," said Smith, "but no one can make an ID. The thieves wore black clothes with stocking masks. They made everyone lie facedown on the floor while Old Man Manicotti cleared out the safe. The best we've got is a woman who smelled Old Spice on one of them—says her husband's worn it for years and she'd know it anywhere."

"Old Spice, eh?" said Loo. (Personally, he preferred Brut.)

The witnesses were still milling around. Loo approached them, speaking to the Old Spice lady and a few others. At the edge of the crowd, he spotted two Buddhist monks in saffron robes.

"What's with them?" he asked. Monks seemed unlikely jewelry shoppers.

"They showed up after it was over," Smith said. "Came up from between those two buildings, the same alley the robbers ran into. We thought they might have seen them with their masks off when they passed."

Loo questioned the monks briefly and then told Smith to arrest them. Why?

315. THE LOST LETTER

Insert the missing letter:

J ? M A M J J A

316. DOUBLE TIME

Here are two puzzles to get your logic muscles working.

1. What do the following words have in common?
Sheath, Pirate, Ashamed, Beauty

2. Which of the following is the odd word out?
Brush, Taste, Shampoo, Stench, Flush, Wash, Seat

317. GREEN, GREEN GRASS

Changing one letter at a time, can you go from GRASS to GREEN in seven steps?

318. HOMOPHONE

Fill in the blanks in the following sentence with three homophone (words that are spelled differently but sound alike). Dashes indicate the number of letters in the words.

If the cut on Jason's _ _ _ _ doesn't _ _ _ _ in time for the big race, _ _ ' _ _ just have to watch from the sidelines.

319. RIDDLERS

1. What can travel around the world while staying in the same corner?

2. What has a mouth but can't chew?

320. TRICKY, TRICKY

Can you think of two words—one meaning "task" and the other meaning "warmth"—that are anagrams of each other?

The cerebellum makes up only 10 percent of the brain's volume…

321. QUICK TRICK

What number comes next in this series?

0 0 1 2 2 4 3 6 4...

322. DOUBLE-SPEAK

Below are five rewritten proverbs. See if you can puzzle out the originals.

1. Each vaporous mass in the firmament contains a metallic interior.

2. Alacrity creates rubbish.

3. An excess of culinary participants impairs the quality of consommé.

4. A mobile piece of petrified matter doesn't aggregate any bryophytes.

5. Noiselessness has an auriferous quality.

323. THE MISSING LETTER

What letter has been omitted from the following?

TBERNTTBE

324. HELLO? HELLO?

Long ago, in the days before cell phones, people actually had to wait in line to use pay phones to make their calls. Take, for example, the five women who were lined up at the phone booth on the corner of Taras and Bulba on this day 20 years ago.

Given the phone records below, can you deduce the order—from first to fifth—in which the women used the phone and to whom each call was made?

1. Immediately after Janelle hung up the phone, someone called the Pizza Palace.

2. Renee's call wasn't to a beauty supply store.

3. In consecutive order, three calls were made: the one to the beauty supply store, a call to a dentist, and Nadia's call.

4. Right after April made her call, another woman called her mother.

5. Matilda didn't make the first call.

6. Nadia's call wasn't to the Pizza Palace.

7. One person called her friend Bella.

325. ONE OF A KIND

The following number is the only one of its kind. Can you figure out what is so special about it? 8,549,176,320.

326. TRICKY MATH

The equation shown below is incorrect, as you can plainly see:

$$5 + 5 + 5 = 550$$

The question is, can you make the equation correct by placing just one line somewhere in it? (And we don't mean putting a line through the equal sign to make it a "does not equal" sign.)

327. QUICK TRICK

Can you, by adding one line, turn these numbers into a time of day?

10 10 10

328. WHAT'S THE WORD?

What palindromic word is referred to in this classic verse?

> Pronounced as one letter but written with three,
> only two different letters are used to make me,
> I'm double, I'm single, I'm black, blue, and gray,
> I'm read from both ends and the same either way.

329. WORD LADDER

Go from RIVER to SHORE in 11 steps.

330. A DEATH IN THE FAMILY

Dick and Jane lay dead on the living-room floor. There were no obvious signs of foul play and no other indications of the cause of death. The only thing unusual about the scene was a wet carpet underneath the bodies.

The only ones home were the cleaning lady and the family's Labrador retriever. The cleaning lady swore she was innocent, and indeed, she had been the one to find the bodies.

How did Dick and Jane die?

Highest score in tournament Scrabble: Joyce Canfield posted 885 points in 1986.

331. HERE FISHY, FISHY

Move three toothpicks to turn the fish around.
(Don't overlap or break any.)

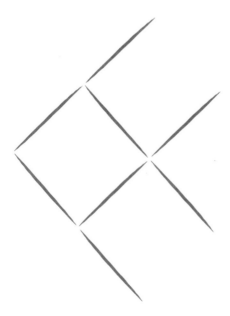

Dodgers pitcher Kevin Brown holds a B.S. in chemical engineering from Georgia Tech.

332. LET'S GET DIVISIVE

Can you divide 110 into two numbers so that one is 150 percent of the other?

333. FIND THE COUNTERFEIT

A counterfeit coin among 12 genuine coins can be detected only by its weight—it's either heavier or lighter than the others. By using a balance scale, how is it possible to identify the counterfeit coin in only three operations?

334. LETTER PLAY

Where does the letter P belong? Above or below the line?

G J Q Y
_____
A B C D E F H I K L M N O R S T U V W X Z

Thomas Jefferson personally designed his Virginia home, Monticello.

335. ANAGRAM THIS

See if you can fill in the blanks below with the two missing words that are anagrams of each other. The number of dashes corresponds to the number of letters in the words.

Experienced classroom _ _ _ _ _ _ _ _ are usually pretty good at recognizing kids who are _ _ _ _ _ _ _ _.

336. RIDDLER

What does a dog do that a man slips on?

337. FEEDING TIME

Employees at Pete's Pets have to feed all of the animals in the morning, following a strict schedule. Can you figure out who gets fed when?

1. The fish are fed before the puppies but after the cats.

2. The birds are fed 15 minutes after the cats.

3. The snakes are fed after the puppies.

Birdbrain? The Clark's nutcracker can remember the locations of 30,000 buried seeds.

338. WHO SNATCHED MRS. MURGATROYD'S PURSE?

Three people witnessed a purse-snatching incident, and each claims to know who did it. However, they don't seem to be able to agree on the identity of the guilty party. Each witness fingers a different culprit, all three of whom are known criminals with a history of just this type of activity.

To add to the confusion, each of the witnesses has made three statements, but two of them made no true statements—and the truthfulness of the third witness is unknown. Can you help bring the perpetrator to justice?

Witness A

1. I saw Gus do it.

2. Bluto did not do it.

3. Big Al wouldn't do something like that.

Witness B

1. A's second statement is false.

2. Bluto did it.

3. Like me, Gus is an upstanding citizen.

Witness C

1. Big Al is the culprit.

2. B's statements are all true.

3. I agree with A's second statement.

Q: What computer language was named for a French mathematician? A: PASCAL

339. WILD & WOOLLY WORDY

Can you figure out what word or phrase this stands for?

T_RN

340. BARBERSHOP QUIZTET

You're sitting in a barber chair having your hair cut. You look in the mirror and can read the word BARBER painted on the shop window behind you. How does the word appear to people outside the shop?

341. NATURAL RESOURCES

Can you turn OIL into GAS in five steps by changing one letter at a time, and using common English words each time?

First spacecraft to land on the moon: the Soviet probe *Luna 2* in 1959.

342. TEASER

Imagine that you're in a sinking rowboat that's surrounded by sharks. How could you possibly survive?

343. NUMBERS IN A SEQUENCE

Which set of numbers would most logically come next in the following sequence?

10 1 9 2 8 3 7 4 6 5 5 6 4 7 3 8 2

a. 9 1   c. 8 5
b. 9 3   d. 6 7

344. LANGUAGE EQUATION

If "16 = O in a P stands for 16 ounces in a pound," what does this equation stand for?

365 = D in a Y

345. WONDERFUL WORDPLAY

Uncle Todd likes indigo but not blue, onions but not turnips, forms but not shapes. According to the same rule, does he like athletes or sports figures?

346. THE HIDDEN MESSAGE

We think there's some industrial sabotage going on here. Can you find a hidden message in this memo?

> Markson is insisting that the second key to the office supplies cabinet and the two colored transparencies will first need clearance before Kenton and Philpott arrive at the office to check all the material early next Monday, so that Peterson can develop them on Tuesday afternoon and take them over to Davidoff's department on Wednesday morning.

347. AND THE NUMBER IS?

What number should replace the question mark below?

$$
\begin{array}{cccc}
6 & 3 & 4 & 5 \\
4 & 5 & 7 & 4 \\
8 & 3 & 4 & 7 \\
3 & 9 & 6 & ?
\end{array}
$$

348. TAKING THE TOUR

Circle Island has sightseeing boats that leave from the same dock and travel around the island in opposite directions. The boats leave the dock every 15 minutes: on the hour, 15 minutes past, half past, and 45 minutes past. The clockwise boats take two hours for the trip, and the counterclockwise boats take three hours.

If two tourists set out at the same time traveling in opposite directions, how many boats will each traveler see on the tour, including the boats they see at the starting point and the ones on which they are traveling?

TV engineer Charles Douglass invented the sitcom laugh track in 1953.

349. COLOR COORDINATION

If green + blue = 89 and red + brown = 98, what will yellow + black make?

350. EUREKA!

Can you turn ROCK into GOLD in five steps, changing one letter at a time and using common English words each time?

351. WILD & WOOLLY WORDY

Can you figure out what word or phrase this stands for?

NA NA FISH

What's so special about March 14? It's Pi day! (3/14)

352. MURDER AT THE B&B

Trouble seemed to follow Inspector Commodius Loo—even on vacation. He was on Long Island's South Shore, hoping to do some deep-sea fishing, when a murder at the B&B where he was staying interfered. Loo had just returned after downing a few Guinnesses at a nearby bar when the proprietors asked for his help.

"I heard the shot at 12:15 a.m.," Mrs. Barlow told him. "I was sitting at my vanity table brushing my hair and putting on moisturizer."

Her husband nodded. "I was in bed reading," Mr. Barlow confirmed.

"Are you sure of the time?" The inspector asked. He had left the bar at midnight and was back in his room shortly thereafter. A shot at 12:15 would have grabbed his attention. But he hadn't heard one.

"Positive," Mrs. Barlow said. "I was so shocked that I looked up from what I was doing, glanced up and distinctly saw the face of our grandfather clock reflected in the mirror. It clearly read 12:15."

Sirens sounded in the night.

"The cops are here," Inspector Loo said. "Now I know what time to tell them the shot was fired."

What time did Mrs. Barlow actually hear the shot?

A border collie named Betsy recognizes 300 different words and fetches toys by name.

353. UPHILL AND DOWNHILL: A CLASSIC PUZZLE BY LEWIS CARROLL

Two travelers spend from 3:00 till 9:00 walking along a level road, up a hill, and back home again. Their pace on the level road was four miles an hour, three miles an hour on the uphill road, and six miles an hour downhill. Find the distance walked and (within half an hour) the time each reached the top of the hill.

354. CALENDAR DAZE

If a certain month has five Thursdays in it and the date of the second Friday is the 11th...

1. What's the date of the third Tuesday?

2. What's the date of the last Friday in the month?

3. What's the date of the first Monday in the month?

4. How many Saturdays are in the month?

5. What's the date of the last Sunday in the month?

First commercial satellite to be launched: AT&T's *Telstar 1*, in 1962.

355. GOING GREEK

What word can be placed inside the brackets that has the same meaning as the words outside?

GREEK GODDESS [_ _ _ _] PONDER

356. LIKE CLOCKWORK

The great two-ton Detroit clock was the hit of the 1876 Centennial Exhibition in Philadelphia. Not only did it give the time in 13 cities, but it kept track of the seasons and plotted the orbits of the planets around the sun. It also inspired the following problem. How many times do the clock's hands meet between noon and midnight?

357. WHAT'S THE WORD?

Can you think of a six-letter word made up of only the following four letters?

L I E G

358. QUICK ID

Eight guys entered a lineup at the police station, walking in one behind the other. There were two places between Fats and Ernesto. Gerhard was immediately in front of Hank. Cecil was three places in front of Dennis and there were two places between Drew and Bruce. Bruce was somewhere in front of Fats, Hank was somewhere in front of Cecil, and Ernesto was immediately in front of Drew. Before they even had a chance to turn to the two-way mirror, the witness identified the fourth from the front as the criminal the police were looking for. What was his name?

359. UNSCRAMBLE IT!

Here's an anagram of the word that holds the record for the highest-scoring opening in Scrabble: QIBUZSEE. Can you figure out the word? (Hint: It's a card game.)

...Ken Jennings correctly answered about 2,700 questions.

360. LANGUAGE EQUATION

If 16 = O. in a P. stands for 16 ounces in a pound, what does this equation stand for?

7 = W of the W

361. BAGS OF TRICKS

On the game show *Gimme a Lotta Money*, the final round was set up thusly: Three treasure chests are labeled DOLLARS, DOUGHNUTS, and ONE OF EACH. Of course, nothing is as easy as it seems—all three chests are mislabeled.

One chest contains two bags of dollars, another chest two bags of doughnuts, and the third chest contains one bag of dollars and one bag of doughnuts. The contestant is allowed to open only one bag of only one chest, after which he or she has to select one and only one chest to take home.

If you were the contestant, which treasure chest would you choose to open, assuming you wanted to go home with the two bags of dollars?

362. WORD LADDER

Can you go from EAST to EDEN in 10 steps?

While testing radar in 1946, Edwin Armstrong bounced FM radio waves off the moon.

363. BOOK LEARNIN'

A man walked up to a woman behind a counter and handed her a book. The woman took it and said, "That'll be $3.25." The man gave her the money and walked out; the woman kept the book. Why?

364. TEASERS

1. Your friendly neighborhood butcher is 6'2". What does he weigh?

2. Would you rather a crocodile attacked you or an alligator?

365. TRICKY, TRICKY

Can you think of a word that's an anagram of itself? If you can do that seemingly impossible feat, you might try thinking of a second word that's an anagram of itself.

Answers

1. HIGH SCHOOL REUNION

	Surname	Claim to Fame	Occupation
Sophie	Mayer	Most Likely to Succeed	Computer programmer
Heather	Mulroney	Class Clown	Dentist
Binky	Moskowitz	Valedictorian	Lawyer
Zoe	French	Most School Spirit	Financial consultant

• According to statements 2 and 5, Binky is Moskowitz, and Heather is Mulroney. From statement 3, Zoe, who isn't Mayer, is French. Therefore, Sophie is Mayer, the computer programmer.

• Statement 6 tells us that Heather, who isn't the lawyer, the financial consultant, or the computer programmer, is the dentist; and from statement 4, she was the Class Clown.

• According to statement 1, Zoe French was not Most Likely to Succeed or valedictorian, and since she wasn't a Class Clown, she had to have had Most School Spirit. From statement 4, Zoe is the financial consultant. Therefore, Binky Moskowitz is the lawyer and was the valedictorian. Sophie Mayer was the Most Likely to Succeed.

2. CONNECT THE STARS

There are 11 squares total: 5 small ones, 4 medium ones, and 2 large ones.

3. GONE FISHIN'

Roberto, using worms, caught one fish. Adam, using dry flies, caught three fish. Oscar, using bacon, caught two fish. Eddie, using bologna, caught no fish at all.

4. WHAT'S THE WORD?

LONG: LONG-DISTANCE, LONG JUMP, LONGHORN, LONGBOW, LONG-WINDED

5. INSPECTOR LOO AND THE BUMBLING ARCHAEOLOGIST

Inspector Loo knew right away that the local guide had pulled the wool over Kansas's eyes. An actual ancient coin would not be dated "BC." There was no such thing as BC until the advent of the era known as AD.

6. TODAY'S THE DAY

Monday

7. WHAT HAPPENS IN VEGAS

Oswald (lost $2401) is married to Betty (won $2601)
Bernard (lost $529) is married to Belinda (won $729)
Harry (lost $25) is married to Vera (won $225).

8. WILD & WOOLLY WORDY Made in China

9. CRIMINOLOGY

Nora is innocent because she says so twice. That means
Nick's statement (9) is a lie, so his other two statements
must be true. Since (8) is true, (15) is a lie, which means
that (14) is true and Jane is the thief.

10. DINNER'S ON By serving mashed potatoes.

11. ACEY-DEUCEY   A A 2 A A 2 2 2

12. SUMMER AT CAMP MANY-HAHAS

Gracie Bernstein is 14, Katie Garcia is 13, and Peter Klein
is 12.

13. QUICK TRICK

7-22-13. This is a simple substitution cryptogram in
which you substitute letters for numbers:
8 = S, 22 = E, 7 = T, etc.

14. TRIPLETS

Square the first number (2 x 2 = 4) and add 1 to get the second number (4 + 1 = 5). Double the middle number to get the last number (5 x 2 = 10). So the last three sets look like this:

$$5 \quad 26 \quad 52$$
$$6 \quad 37 \quad 74$$
$$7 \quad 50 \quad 100$$

15. WORD GAME

Tuesday, Thursday, today, and tomorrow!

16. IT'S SYMBOLIC

The message is made up of equations that include judgments about their correctness as follows:

$$1 + 2 = 3 \qquad \text{true}$$
$$2 + 2 = 4 \qquad \text{true}$$
$$3 + 2 = 4 \qquad \text{false}$$

The empty circles stand for numbers; the filled circles stand for "+"; the star stands for "="; the upside-down U stands for "true"; and the regular U stands for "false."

17. COMPARING APPLES AND SISTERS

Angela Jackson, Marcy Redfield, Janette Smythe, and Kristen Brownfield

18. DEAR OLD DAD

The difference between the ages is 23 years, so I must be 23 if my father is twice as old (46).

19. WILD & WOOLLY WORDY

Slow down.

20. WHERE THERE'S A WILL...

The two fathers and two sons refer to only three people: a grandfather, his son (who is also a father), and his son.

21. INSPECTOR LOO AND THE STRANGER

The man knocked first. He wouldn't have done that if he had really believed it was his room.

22. THE SAME GAME

They all come in pairs.

23. OINK, OINK, OUCH!

You have 35 quarters ($8.75), 9 dimes (90 cents), 6 nickels (30 cents), and 5 pennies (5 cents).

24. CHOO-CHOO!

6,477

25. MYSTERY MATH

```
  444
  444
   44
   44
    4
    4
    4
    4
    4
+   4
1,000
```

26. WHAT'S THE WORD?

TURN: TURNTABLE, TURN UP, TURN TAIL, TURNPIKE, TURNOVER

27. HERE'S LOOKING AT YOU, KID

The women, now grown, had been classmates in kindergarten.

28. RAPID FIRE

• If you think that you are now in first place, think again! If you overtake the person in second place, you are now in second place yourself!

• One thousand

29. TRICKY TRIANGLES

57. Multiply the left number in each triangle by the square of the right number. Then divide by the bottom number.

30. RODEO ROUNDUP

The men placed like this:

1: Wes Podunk, newspaper editor, Trigger

2: Moose Jessup, dentist, Kickapoo

3: Duke Washburton, corporate lawyer, Arbuckle

4: Jake Slaughter, radio show host, Dusty

5: Rusty Canter, factory foreman, Goldie

6: Steve Burly, florist, Pardner

31. A SAFE PLACE

Fred is playing baseball and the masked man is the catcher.

32. MADE IN THE USA
STAEX = TEXAS
IHGCCOA = CHICAGO
GOYIWMN = WYOMING
IMENA = MAINE

33. SOCK IT TO ME

Mr. Rose didn't wear rose or olive socks; therefore, his have to be ivory. Mr. Olive's socks can't be olive, so they must be rose. That leaves Mr. Ivory with the olive socks.

34. IT FIGURES

A left-pointing arrow. The pattern starts with three black diamonds interspersed with white figures, and then it begins again with the same figures reversed.

35. THE INSPECTOR SOLVES A KIDNAPPING CASE

Terry's story had a few holes. He told Loo he had seen his attacker only from the back. If so, he would not have known his sweatshirt zipped up the front. Terry ultimately confessed that he and Tony had concocted the whole kidnapping scheme to bilk their father out of a million dollars.

36. WONDERFUL WORDPLAY

Dart, match, fire

37. I'LL TAKE ROMANCE

Clue 1 tells us that the middle book is purple, Barbara Musk wrote the book on the right, and *Long Nights* is the book on the left. Therefore, the book by Rosamund Fahrquar is in the middle because it's to the right of a book (clue 2), and we know that Barbara Musk wrote the book on the right. We can also deduce that the puce book is on the left. By process of elimination, the fuchsia book is on the right. According to clue 3, Danielle Skweel must have written the book on the left, so *Shining Armor* is in the middle and *Heart on Fire* is on the right.

The books line up from left to right like this:

Long Nights, Danielle Skweel, puce

Shining Armor, Rosamund Fahrquar, purple

Heart on Fire, Barbara Musk, fuchsia

38. LOGIC BY THE NUMBERS

18 is the only even multiple of 9 between 10 and 22.
Check it out: 18 x 4½ = 81.

39. THE LUNCHTIME CROWD

First name	Last name	Sandwich	Side dish	Dessert
Peter	Waller	tofu	baked potato	marionberry pie
Emlyn	Benjamin	turkey	coleslaw	green-tea ice cream
Marco	Wayvern	Spam	garden salad	hot-fudge sundae
Walter	Hanks	roast beef	rice pilaf	chocolate cake

40. THE MAGIC NUMBER

No solution necessary.

41. RAPID FIRE

• Wrong

• 70. 30 divided by 2 would have made a total of 25, but
30 divided by ½ = 60, plus 10 = 70.

• A dozen of anything is still 12.

42. THINK ABOUT IT

They're the remains of a melted snowman.

43. WHAT'S THE WORD?

Fruit

44. WILD & WOOLLY WORDY

A walk in the park

45. IT'S HISTORY

Read the first line of the first verse, then the first line of
the second verse, the second line of the first verse, then
the second line of the second verse, and so on.

> The pomps of Courts and pride of kings
> I fain would banish far from hence.
> I prize above all earthly things;
> The 'Rights of Man' and 'Common Sense.'
> I love my country, but the King,
> Confusion to his odious reign.
> Above all men, his praise I sing.
> That foe to princes, Thomas Paine.
> The Royal banners are displayed,
> Defeat and ruin seize the cause.
> And may success the standard aid
> Of France, its liberties and laws.

The author escaped to France in 1807, where he became a
general in Napoléon's army, and died at age 87.

46. GETTING AWAY WITH MURDER

The brothers were conjoined twins.

47. GREEN, GREEN GRASS

Solution: Here's one way to do it: GRASS, CRASS, CRESS, TRESS, TREES, TREED, GREED, GREEN.

48. A WEIGHTY PROBLEM

Jim can use two scales: placing one foot on each scale, he can add the results together.

49. GO FIGURE

Turn it upside down; it becomes $8 + 8 = 16$.

50. THE POWER OF 9

Here's how it works: The trick relies on the power of 9. (And a simple knowledge of the 9 times table. See? It's finally coming in handy!)

After the person has added up the digits and done the subtraction, the answer will always be divisible by 9. And if a number divides evenly by 9, when the digits are added up, they will also divide by 9. If you check our example—$5+6+8+0+8 = 27$—you'll see that it divides by 9.

So, after the person crosses out a digit and reads you the digits that are left, you add them up. In this case, $5+8+0+8 = 21$. What's the next number that's divisible by 9? 27. What would you have to add to 21 to get 27? Six! That's the number that was crossed out!

51. FAMILY RELATIONSHIPS   Charlotte is Mitzi's niece.

52. CAPITAL PUN-ISHMENT

Ice cube

53. LETTER PERFECT

In this sentence there are two O's, five T's, and five N's.

54. LO-CAL PIES

Patrice ate three slices of blueberry and once slice of lemon meringue. Bebe ate one of each. Hortense ate one of each. Jeanmarie ate one slice of coconut, two pecan, and one lemon meringue.

55. INSPECTOR LOO AND THE CASE OF THE COLUMNIST

Loo realized that what appeared to be a line of nonsense at the end of the file (49t34 w5qgg3e j3) actually translated as "Roger stabbed me." Mack had managed to type the message after being attacked, but his fingers were positioned one line too high on the keyboard.

56. WHAT'S THE SCOOP?

The correct labels, from left to right, should read: BERRY-BERRY, CHOCOLATE, COCONUT, VANILLA, HAZELNUT.

57. WILD & WOOLLY WORDY

Railroad crossing

58. SEQUENTIAL THINKING

None of the numbers contains an "e" when spelled out in English. The next number will be 2,000.

59. COINS OF THE REALM

There were 3,000 gold coins, 4,000 silver, and 5,000 bronze. Assume each statement to be true in turn and examine the consequences. If the gold coin counter is telling the truth, there are 3,000 silver coins, 5,000 bronze coins, and therefore 4,000 gold coins. But this would make the bronze coin counter's statement true as well; this cannot be since two of the coin counters are lying about at least one of their amounts. So only the silver coin counter's statement is true.

60. INSPECTOR LOO OUTWITS A DEAD MAN

Inspector Loo suggested that the executor put all the money from the liquidation of assets into a separate bank account, and then write a check for the full amount to Uncle Murray, place it in the coffin, and proceed with the cremation. If the check did not get cashed within 30 days, the will would go to probate and the Mayo estate would be evenly divided among the heirs.

61. FLYING FRUITCAKES

Number	Name	Wore	Color
1	Gunther	2	orange
2	Levar	3	lime green
3	Buddy	1	lemon yellow
4	Homer	4	peach

62. CIRCULAR REASONING

2. When added together, the numbers opposite each other equal 13.

63. HOMOPHONES

1. My sister is going on a cruise in the Baltic and Caspian SEAS, but first she'll go to a bargain sale at the travel shop and SEIZE everything she SEES.

2. My brother got so upset when he started going BALD that he sometimes BALLED himself up on the floor and BAWLED his eyes out.

64. LIGHT MY FIRE

Here's one way to do it: FIRE, HIRE, HERE, HERD, HEAD, HEAT.

65. LETTER PERFECT

In this sentence there are three F's, four H's, and five T's.

66. POSTGRADUATE WORK

First Name	Last Name	Summer Job	Major
Marcia	Rankin	carhop	Education
Petula	Spangler	camp counselor	Art
Suzanne	Waring	office worker	French
Winona	Culkin	barista	Physics

67. TREACHEROUS TRAVELING

The woman, who used to be blind, is returning from a Swiss clinic where an operation restored her sight. When the train went through a tunnel, she thought she'd gone blind again and decided to kill herself by jumping off the train. But before she could do it, she saw the lights of the cigarettes people were smoking and realized she could still see.

68. A GOOD GOOD NIGHT

Here's one way to do it: SLEEP, BLEEP, BLEED, BREED, BREAD, DREAD, DREAM.

69. ABANDONED SHIP

The people on the yacht went swimming, but didn't realize that the boat would rise when they all dove into the water. The boat's ladder rose with the boat, and was just out of reach.

70. FIVE-FLOOR WALK-UP

From top floor to bottom: Ivan, Lance, Andrea, Olivia, and Max.

71. WHAT'S THE WORD?

1. DOWN: DOWNDRAFT, DOWNFALL, DOWNGRADE, DOWNHILL, DOWNLOAD, DOWNRIGHT

2. DOUBLE: DOUBLE AGENT, DOUBLE-CROSS, DOUBLE DRIBBLE, DOUBLE JEOPARDY, DOUBLE WHAMMY.

72. AT THE MOVIES

The movie on screen 1 doesn't start at 7:00 (clue 1), 7:30 (2), or 7:10 (3), so it starts at 7:20. *Crash Landing* is on screen 2 (4), starting at 7:10, and the movie on screen 3 starts at 7:00. *Spaceship to Nowhere* is on screen 4 (1) and starts at 7:30. Screen 3 isn't showing *I Married My Sister's Boyfriend* (3), so it's showing *Grammar School Musical*. Screen 1 is showing *I Married My Sister's Boyfriend*. Here's the schedule:

Screen 1 – 7:20 – *I Married My Sister's Boyfriend*

Screen 2 – 7:10 – *Crash Landing*

Screen 3 – 7:00 – *Grammar School Musical*

Screen 4 – 7:30 – *Spaceship to Nowhere*

73. SEEK AND FIND

THIS IS A SECRET. (Delete the word CLUE, which appears three times in alternate spaces.)

74. QUITE AN ARRANGEMENT

Just make the 8 and 9 change places. First turn the 9 upside so it becomes a 6. Then swap the 8 and the 6. Then, each column will add up to 18.

75. MAKE MINE A DOUBLE

Joe went into the coffee shop hiccuping loudly. The gun scared the hiccups out of him.

76. ECHOES

Whale wail

77. ABOVE OR BELOW

The 9 and 10 go below the line. Numbers with curved lines go below the line; those with straight lines go above.

78. INSPECTOR LOO AND THE FIRING SQUAD

Inspector Loo had them form a circle around him. With everyone facing in at Loo, ready to shoot, they realized that those who missed would likely hit somebody else around the perimeter, so no one dared to fire.

79. WILD & WOOLLY WORDY
Double Vision

80. ANAGRAM THIS
1. mile, lime   **2.** tool, loot.

81. RIDDLER
A cheetah

82. WHAT A WAY TO GO
The man stowed away in the landing gear compartment of a jet, died of hyperthermia midflight, and fell out when the compartment opened as the plane made its final approach to the airport.

83. ROPE SWING
Tie the scissors to one of the ropes and make it move like a pendulum. Then take the other end of the rope and grab the scissors as they come toward you. Then tie the knot.

84. SUCCESS STORY
Here's one way to do it: POOR, POOL, POLL, POLE, PILE, RILE, RICE, RICH.

85. I SPY

If there's only one double agent, Boris is it. Both Anastasia and Natasha are telling the truth. So, when Anastasia said, "Boris is a double agent," she was telling the truth, and gave you the correct answer. When Boris said, "Natasha is a double agent," he was lying, as he himself is a lying double agent. When Natasha responded, "Boris is lying," she was telling the truth, and also affirming that Boris was lying.

If, on the other hand, there were two double agents, both Anastasia and Natasha would be double agents, and Boris would be telling the truth.

86. RUSHED TO THE HOSPITAL

The wearing of seat belts was successful in reducing the number of deaths from road accidents. The accident victims who wore seat belts ended up at the hospital instead of the morgue. Consequently, more people were treated for injuries than before.

87. TOM SWIFTY

1. g ("A thousand thanks, Monsieur," Tom said mercifully.)

2. c ("Don't you like my new refrigerator," Tom asked coolly.)

3. f ("I prefer t press my own clothes," Tom said ironically.)

4. h ("I'll have to send that telegram again," Tom said remorsefully.)

5. j ("I'm burning the candle at both ends," Tom said wickedly.)

6. e ("It's the maid's night off," Tom said helplessly.)

7. a ("The boat is leaking," Tom said balefully.)

8. b ("The criminals were escorted downstairs," Tom said condescendingly.)

9. i ("They pulled the wool over my eyes," Tom said sheepishly.)

10. d ("Welcome to Grant's Tomb," Tom said cryptically.)

88. THE FOUR DOSSIERS

Horace Rivers is the polo player, and therefore the double agent. The dossiers contain this information:

A, Justin Edwards, golf pro

B, Horace Rivers, polo player

C, Ralph Grimes, missionary

D, Manfred von Troganoff, business consultant

89. WILD & WOOLLY WORDY

Life begins at 40.

90. PENGUINS ON PARADE

Volkswagen: 24

Hummer: 96

Falcon: 40

Civic: 64

Mercedes: 112

91. DECISIONS, DECISIONS

Beet Red. From left to right, the cars are Snowy White, Bottle Green, Midnight Black, Beet Red, Hi-Ho Silver, Sunny Yellow, Sky Blue, and Royal Purple.

92. ONE FOR THE AGES

She'll be 17 in seven years.

93. SOCRATES SPEAKS

In every second row, some of the letters differ from those in the row above it. Those letters spell out this message: "There is only one good—knowledge—and one evil—ignorance." —*Socrates*

94. THREE TO FOUR

95. ANAGRAM THIS
1. That queer shake
2. Bad credit
3. Here come dots

96. AIR TRAFFIC
Barbara already knew about the crash—the movie she was watching had been taped two nights earlier.

97. OOPS!
It was winter. He fired the gun near a snowy cliff, which started an avalanche.

98. ALL JAZZED UP
Angelina: "Lullaby of Broadway"
Candy: "It's De-Lovely"
Martha: "When Sunny Gets Blue"
Germaine: "Autumn Leaves"
Stella: "In the Mood"

99. THE FIVE NEWSBOYS BY SAM LOYD (1841–1911)
The Jones boys sold 220 more papers than the Smith boys. The original number of papers was 1,020.

100. AUTHOR OF THE YEAR
First: Henry Austen – Mike Wrench

Second: Nancy Pickle – Jeanette Heat

Third: Chet Fong – Parker Van Dine

Fourth: Barry Tisdale – Herman Medville

101. SEQUENTIAL THINKING

The name of each number gives the first letter of the next highest whole number: zerO, OnE, EighT, TeN, NineteeN, NinetY. There are no numbers in the English language that begin with Y.

102. TRICKY Joe was reading in Braille.

103. WILD AND WOOLLY WORDY Upside down.

104. A NIGHT AT THE ROUND TABLE

• Roger is Winona's husband. From statement 2, we know that the six people sat at the table in the following way (clockwise and starting with Winona's husband): Winona's husband, woman, man, woman, man, Esther

• Because Winona did not sit beside her husband (4), the situation must be as follows: Winona's husband, woman, man, Winona, man, Esther

• The remaining woman must be Nicole, and figuring in statement 1, the configuration must be: Winona's husband, Nicole, man, Winona, Victor, Esther

• Because of statement 3, Manny and Roger can be placed in only one way: Winona's husband Roger, Nicole, Manny, Winona, Victor, Esther

105. POOL SHARK

It will end up in one of the pockets, though not the one it started from.

106. THE LOGICAL NUMBER

The missing number is 6. The number in the middle of each set is the same as the sum of the digits of the first and last numbers: for example, 3 + 7 = 10 = 8 + 2.

107. WHAT'S THE DEAL?

You can continue the deal by taking cards from the bottom of the deck, dealing first to yourself, then counterclockwise around the table.

108. EVOLUTION

Here's one way to do it: APE, APT, OPT, OAT, MAT, MAN.

109. YOU DO THE MATH

Eight. There were 48 states before Alaska, four seasons, 40 thieves, and 29 days in February in a leap year. Two cubed is eight.

110. PUZZLE IT OUT   2 and 4

111. ODD MAN OUT

1. 63120. In the other four, the first three numbers added together make the last two.

2. 8421. The other six are pairs in which the third and

second digits are followed by the fourth and first.

3. 13. In the other four, cube the last digit to get the first ones.

4. 8609. In the other four, the first and last numbers multiplied together give you the second and third.

112. SHAPE UP!

⬟ = 1

▢ = 2

⬤ = 3

◇ = 4

$$2 + 2$$
$$2 + 2 + 4$$
$$3 + 3 + 3 + 1$$
$$4 + 4 + 1 + 4$$
$$\underline{3 + 3 + 2 + 2}$$
$$1 \quad 1 \quad 3 \quad 1 \quad 3$$

113. CONGA!

1. Ollie – art department

2. Vern – art department

3. Patsy – sales

4. Elwood – art department

5. Rickie – art department

6. Helen – sales

7. Darla – art department

8. Tori – editor

9. Binky – sales

10. Zoe – art department

11. Gerard – art department

12. Fantasia – sales

13. Beau – art department

14. Donnie – editor

15. Cookie – sales

114. ANAGRAM THIS Retain, retina

115. WILD & WOOLLY WORDY Space Invaders

116. FOUR SQUARE

1.

2.

3.

4.

5.

6.

117. NOW THAT'S A CLASSIC

He said, "I will be hanged." If he were hanged, it would be the truth, and if they tickled him to death, it would be a lie, so they set him free.

118. NICE NUMBERS

NINETY = 848015. (TWELVE = 130760, THIRTY = 194215)

119. GUILTY OR INNOCENT   Kim

120. THE THREE TRAVELERS

The plan adopted is as follows:

1. Two of the servants are sent over.

2. One of the servants brings back the boat, and takes over the third servant.

3. Once of the servants brings the boat back, lands, and two of the masters go over.

4. One of the masters and one of the servants return, the servant lands, and the third master crosses with the second. The position of matters is now as follows: The three masters are on the farther side with one of the servants, who is sent back with the boat, and fetches, one at a time, the other two servants.

121. RULES, SCHMULES

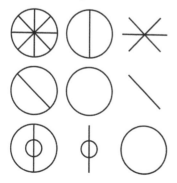

122. NOUVEAU RICH!

Ariana Sargent, Salinas, take a trip around the world

Jasper Postner, Merced, build a house

Miranda Caruso, Daly City, quit her job

Ramona Mooney, Chico, redecorate her house

Tex Peterson, Mariposa, pay off debts

123. DON'T PUT THE CART BEFORE THE PONY

Here's one way to do it: PONY, PUNY, PUNT, PANT, PART, CART.

124. THE MISSING WORD

The word is SENIOR. Three letters of the left and right words transfer to the middle as follows:

```
R I N S E D
6     1 2
[S E N I O R]
 1 2 3 4 5 6
N O V I C E
3 5     4
```

125. WILD AND WOOLLY WORDY Life after death

126. CHRISTMAS IN MONEYED MEADOWS

Swimming pool for the family dog, $20,000, Ewing

Household robot, $12,000, Pirrip

Villa on Capri, $10,000, Carnegie

Nip and tucks, $6,000, Astin

Andy Warhol drawing, $5,000, Forbes

127. TEASER Add a hole.

128. CUT!
You will have three pieces of paper after the cut. Don't believe it? Now go get the paper and scissors and give it a try.

129. LANGUAGE EQUATION
9 justices on the Supreme Court

130. MAGIC NINE

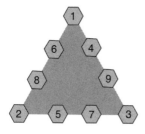

131. A FRIENDLY GET-TOGETHER
Since Donald is speaking to the botanist, and Allison is sitting next to the chemist and across from the dog walker, Caterina must be the anthropologist, and Allison is the botanist. The dog walker didn't speak at all, but Donald did. So Ben is the dog walker and Donald is the chemist.

132. TIME FOR SCHOOL
Henry's time categories overlap so that the same periods of

time are counted more than once. For example, he counted the 45 days he spent eating and the 122 days he slept in addition to the 60 days he was on vacation, even though the eating and sleeping took place during the vacation time. The same was true of his weekends, and so on.

133. A CLASSIC

The letter L

134. THE GANG'S ALL HERE

Gunman: Junior, short, bald.

Lookout: Phil, medium height, blue Mohawk.

Driver: Lefty, tall, gray-haired.

Statement 1 says that the gunman is shorter than the lookout, so the gunman must be either the short or the medium one, and the lookout is either the medium or the tall one. Statements 2 and 3 say Phil is shorter than one man (the driver) and taller that the other (the bald guy), so Phil must be medium height. Therefore, the driver must be the tall one and the bald guy must be the short one. Since the driver is the tall one, the lookout must be medium height, and the gunman must be the short one, as well as the bald guy. Statement 4 says Lefty is taller than the one with the blue Mohawk. Therefore, the blue Mohawk can't be the tall one, and is not the bald, short one (according to Statement 3), so he must be medium height, i.e., Phil. Therefore, Lefty is the tall one with gray hair.

135. LIES, ALL LIES

Pat. If the statement "I did not break the window" is definitely false, we can be certain that Pat broke the window. Statements that some individuals "couldn't have" broken the window only mean that these individuals could have broken the window, but do not guarantee that they did. James's statement that "Paul is innocent" comes with the corollary "I broke the window," which is false and so negates the rest of his statement.

136. HAPPY COUPLES

Nell is married to Edwin, Ursula is married to Lonnie, Helena is married to Mark.

137. A NIGHT OUT IN HOLLYWOOD

Club Three. If the Club One bouncer lies, then Veronica is in Club Two. If the Club Two bouncer lies, Veronica is in Club One. If the Club Three bouncer tells the truth, Veronica is in Club One or Two, and the other two lie. However, this means that Veronica is in both Club One and Two, which is not possible. So the Club Three bouncer lies, implying that Veronica is in Club Three, and there are not two liars at all—just one.

138. WILD AND WOOLLY WORDY

Cabinet

139. WAY OFF-BROADWAY

Tuesday: *Bye-Bye Birdfood,* Bernstein, "Surrey with the Flange on Top"

Wednesday: *Kiss Me Katz,* Coward, "Ol' Man Swimming Pool"

Thursday: *Fiddler on the Hoof,* Sondheim, "Gee, Officer Crumbcake"

Friday: *Auntie Mamie,* Kern, "I'm Gonna Wash My Hair Right Offa My Head"

140. GOOD GROOMING

Here's one way to do it:
COMB, COME, HOME, HOLE, HALE, HALL,
HAIL, HAIR.

141. THINK ON IT

30. In each set, the center number is arrived at by taking the difference between the two numbers on the left, dividing that number by two, then multiplying the result by the sum of the two numbers on the right.

142. PREFERENCES

A star. He only likes words that spell other words backward; e.g., pots/stop, pans/snap, etc.

143. DON'T BE SUCH A WINO

144. TRICKY NUMBER 9

Here's how you do it: Simply multiply the middle number by 9. In this case, the answer is 90. You can hand your friend a calculator to check your answer, but it will work every time.

We'll admit that it gets harder for you, the magician, if they choose, a box in which the center number is something like 23, but here's a handy tip: Multiply the number by 10, then subtract the number. In this case, 23 x 10 = 230; 230 - 23 = 207. With a little bit of practice, you'll be able to do it quickly in your head.

145. BROTHERLY LOVE

According to statement 4, the same two brothers were involved in the Blink's armored truck job and the Adorable You Boutique break-in. Burly was not at the Adorable You Boutique break-in, so he was not at the Blink's job. And since he was not at the Hiawatha Casino caper, he took part in none of the robberies. Earl and Merle committed all three.

146. WILD AND WOOLLY WORDY

Ambiguous

147. QUICK TRICK

I belongs below the line. A, H, J, and K have an "A" sound when pronounced—a feature that the other letters lack.

148. SYBIL'S SIBLINGS

Four sisters and three brothers.

149. UPS AND DOWNS

The nurse was very short and couldn't reach above the button for the eighth floor.

150. BETTER THAN NONE

The bakery started out the morning with 15 loaves of bread. Rachel bought 8, Howie bought 4, Nina bought 2, and Marshall bought 1.

151. NOT A NUMBER PUZZLE

The only vowel they contain when written out is the letter E.

152. CONNECT THE SQUARES

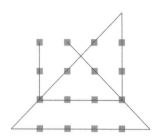

153. INSPECTOR LOO SOLVES THE "LIPSTICK ON HIS COLLAR" CASE

The mailman. He made reference to the fact that Jones was attacked when coming home, something no one except the girlfriend—and the killer—would know for sure. As far as anyone else knew, he could just as easily have been leaving the house as returning to it.

154. FLAMING FLAMINGOS

No. 24. The pattern: $4 \times 4 = 16 - 4 = 12 \div 4 = 3 + 4 = 7 \times 4 = 28 - 4 = 24$.

155. LITTLE GREEN (AND YELLOW AND ORANGE AND PURPLE) MEN

ARRIVED	NAME	COLOR	PLANET	DISTANCE
First	Omina-omina	Yellow	Qiprisca	40
Second	Treb	Orange	Zalkie	16
Third	Wawacha	Purple	Chawawa	31
Fourth	Lufgara	Green	Borkfar	32

156. WHO'S YOUR DADDY?

The friend Penny met up with is a man named Jack. Most people assume that Penny's friend is a woman, even though there's nothing to indicate this is in the puzzle.

157. WILD & WOOLLY WORDY

Thundercloud

158. WHAT'S GONE MISSING?

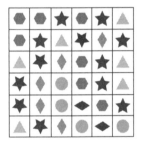

159. LET'S GET BEAUTIFUL

Barney Iverson: conditioner and bikini wax

Amanda O'Brien: hair spray

Chuck Feinstein: shampoo

Terence Friedman: tweezers and facial masks

Chita Draper: nail polish and hair clips

Babs Parker: massage oil

160. LETTER PLAY

T would be on the top row, where all the letters have at least one complete vertical line.

161. PREFERENCES

Aunt Jenny likes words that have double letters: baLLet sliPPers, etc.

162. AT THE CROSSROADS

You could stand the signpost up so that the arm indicating the place you just came from is pointing in the right direction. The other arms will then point in the right direction.

163. TRANSATLANTIC FLIGHT

Don't hire him! "Direct flights" between two places at different latitudes over the Earth's spherical surface usually looked curved when projected onto flat maps. A real pilot wouldn't have plotted a flight plan using a ruler.

164. HIGH NOON

The sun was at 90 degrees at high noon; later, when the shadows were equal in length to the height of the poles, the sun must have been at a 45-degree angle to the ground. Taking into account that the Earth rotates at one degree every four minutes, and that 4 x 45 = 180 (minutes), help arrived at 3:00 p.m.

165. CHERRY PAIRS

14 cherries; 7 pairs. You would have given the 14 cherries to your friends as follows: To the first friend (half of 7) 3½ pairs + ½ a pair = 4 pairs (leaving 3 pairs). To the second friend (half of 3) 1½ pairs + ½ a pair = 2 pairs (leaving 1 pair). To the third friend (half of 1) ½ a pair + ½ a pair = 1 pair.

166. THE CAPTIVES IN THE TOWER
BY LEWIS CARROLL

The boy descended first, using the cannonball as a counterbalance. The queen and her daughter then took the cannonball out of the upper basket, and the daughter descended, the boy acting as counterbalance. The cannonball was then allowed to run down alone. When it reached the ground, the daughter got into the basket along with the cannonball, and their joint weight acted as counterbalance while the queen descended. The princess then went down, the cannonball ascending. The daughter removed the cannonball and went down alone, her brother ascending. The latter then put the cannonball in the opposite basket, and lowered himself to the ground.

167. YOU'VE GOT THE KEY

Take the 4th, 23rd, and 51st letters of the question "What is the key..." which gives us "THE," and so on. The entire message reads "The clue is in the question."

168. YAY TEAM!

Hermione Dodson: left fielder, .325
Cat Farr: shortstop, .280

Leslie Clements: center fielder, .295

Starr Brooks: right fielder, .310

According to statement 6, Hermione is the center fielder. However, the indication that her batting average is lower than the shortstop's can't be correct, considering statement 1. Statements 3 and 5 are also contradictory to statement 6. Therefore, statement 6 is the false one. From statements 1 and 3, since Leslie is not the shortstop, she is the center fielder who bats .295. From (2) and (4), Leslie must be one of the three players who are neighbors. Therefore Leslie's last name is Clements. From (1) and (4), Cat, whose batting average is 30 points below Starr's, is the shortstop, whose batting average is .280; Starr's batting average is .310. From (2) and (5), Starr's last name is Brooks, and she is the right fielder. From (5), Hermione's last name is not Farr. Therefore, Hermione is Dodson, the left fielder, whose batting average is .325. Cat's surname is Farr.

169. TOP THIS

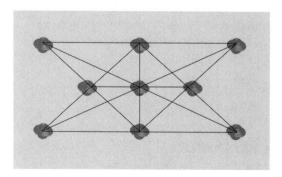

170. THE HONEYMOONERS

- Bart and Deborah Gallagher-Stein, sightseeing, wind chime
- Ed and Sarah Harris-Sanchez, shopping, model ship
- Jake and Tracy Smith-Jones, golfing, T-shirts
- Mel and Cindy Marino-Bork, hiking, postcards
- Thad and Chloe Helm-Danvers, surfing, saltwater taffy

Bart and Deborah (clue 1) Gallagher-Stein (2) went sightseeing (2) and bought the wind chime (5). Jake Smith-Jones (6) went golfing (2) and bought T-shirts (6). Thad went surfing (2). Ed didn't go hiking (4), so by elimination, Ed went shopping and Mel went hiking. Mel bought postcards (6). Ed didn't buy the saltwater taffy (1), so by elimination Thad bought the saltwater taffy and Ed bought the model ship. Therefore, Ed is married to Sarah (5). From (3) and elimination, Cindy is married to Mel and Harris-Sanchez is the last name of Ed and Sarah. Mel's last name is not Helm-Danvers (6), so by elimination, Mel's last name is Marino-Bork, and Thad's is Helm-Danvers. Thad isn't married to Tracy (2), so by elimination, Thad is married to Chloe, and Jake is married to Tracy.

171. SING TO ME
"Happy Birthday"

172. THE FOUR YACHTSMEN
Bentley's dog is Atlas; his yacht is *Hercules*.
Bobby's dog is Hercules; his yacht is *Prince*.

Buford's dog is Prince; his yacht is *Sparky*.

Bradley's dog is Sparky; his yacht is *Atlas*.

173. MONEY TALKS

"Money talks, but to me it says goodbye." Just substitute letters for their numerical place in the alphabet (A = 1, B = 2, etc.).

174. WILD & WOOLLY WORDY Unfinished symphony

175. WHITE HOUSE BOUND You have to be elected.

176. THE DISH

138. Divide the maximum number of dishes, 274, by 2 (because each resident owns an even number and every number is different, e.g., 274, 272, 270, etc.) to get 137. But we have to add 1 to 137 to include 0, which is an even number, in case there was a person who owned no dishes.

177. WILD & WOOLLY WORDY Open and shut case

178. ANCHOR AWAY

The water level would go down. Removing the anchor from the boat will make the boat rise and the water level fall an amount equal to the anchor's weight. When the anchor is then thrown into the water, the level rises an amount equal to the anchor's volume. But because an anchor weighs more than the same volume of water (that's why it sinks), removing the anchor from the boat has a greater effect. Overall, the water level goes down.

179. FOUR DEAD MEN

1. He stood on a block of ice to hang himself, and slowly strangled to death as the ice melted.

2. He stabbed himself with an icicle.

3. He was crossing the dessert in a hot-air balloon with several other people. The balloon began to lose altitude—fast. The passengers drew matches to see who would jump over the side and save the others. This man got the shortest match and had to jump.

4. The drinks contained poisoned ice cubes; the man who drank slowly gave the ice cubes time to melt.

180. TINY BEAUTY QUEENS

From left to right the girls were as follows:

1. Josie, green gown, placed first, popcorn
2. Danielle, red gown, placed fourth, pizza
3. Steffi, blue gown, placed second, hot dogs
4. Tiffany, yellow gown, placed third, nachos

181. STEP AWAY FROM THAT DESK

Here's one way to do it: WORK, WORE, PORE, PORT, PERT, PEAT, FEAT, FLAT, FLAY, PLAY.

If you use the less-than-common word PLAT, you can get there in seven steps: WORK, PORK, PORT, PERT, PEAT, PLAT, PLAY.

182. TRICKY Peacocks don't lay eggs; peahens do.

183. WHAT A GLOW
Here's one way to do it: GLOW, SLOW, SLOT, SOOT, FOOT, FORT, FORM, WORM

184. THE PRICE POINT
$6.50. Consonants are worth $1 each and vowels are worth 50 cents.

185. QUICK TRICK   e) FIG (alphabetical order)

186. THERE SHE IS...
Jenna Watson, Miss New York, deviled eggs

Kate Bronfman, Miss Hawaii, paella

Leslie Darling, Miss California, brownies

Margo Orlando, Miss Texas, fruit salad

Norma Martinez, Miss Pennsylvania, quiche

187. GOT CLUE?
Miss Scarlett, candlestick, kitchen

Professor Plum, rope, study

Colonel Mustard, lead pipe, library

Mrs. White, gun, conservatory

188. WILD & WOOLLY WORDY
One way or the other

189. A SQUARE FULL OF SQUARES

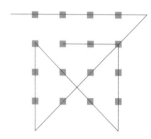

190. A DAY AT THE DENTIST

Rocco Zabriskie, room 103, 3:00 p.m.
Carlotta Schmidt, room 102, 4:00 p.m.
Abigail Nogumi, room 105, 5:00 p.m.
Deborah Jimenez, room 104, 6:00 p.m.

191. WORD LADDER

Here's one way to do it: HEAD, HEAL, TEAL, TELL, TALL, TAIL.

192. AN AGE-OLD QUESTION 80

193. THE TWO TRIBES

"Hubba-hubba" has to mean "yes." If the islander were a truth-teller, he would tell the truth and answer yes; if he were a liar, he would lie and still answer yes. So when the shorter islander told the anthropologist that his companion said "Yes," the short fellow was telling the truth. That means that the rest of his statement was true: the taller fellow was a liar.

194. TEASER

There are two answers to this question. You can have $20.19 without being able to change a twenty: a ten, a five, four ones, three quarters, four dimes, and four pennies. You can also have an infinite amount of money made up of all the bills over $20.

195. TRICKY

Nearly drowned. If you were almost saved, you'd have drowned.

196. ECHOES

Ate eight

197. DANGER!

The contestants finished as follows:

Barry Canales, Pacific Park, $8,000

Justin Rodriguez, Santa Teresa, $5,000

Amy Wong, Forrest Canyon, $4,000

198. INSPECTOR LOO NAILS AN INSIDE JOB

It was the second security guard. He said he was getting the mail, but there is no mail delivery on Sunday.

199. MAGIC RULER

The ruler is marked at 1 inch, 4 inches, 7 inches, and 10 inches. Lengths can be measured like this: 1 inch = 0–1; 2 inches = 10–12; 3 inches = 1–4, 4–7, or 7–10; 4 inches =

0–4; 5 inches = 7–12; 6 inches = 1–7 or 4–10; 8 inches =
4–12; 9 inches = 1–10; 11 inches = 1–12; 12 inches =
0–12.

200. YO-HO-HO!

120. If you add all the fractions plus 10 plus 1, letting x =
the number of coins found, it looks like this:

$\frac{x}{3} + \frac{x}{4} + \frac{x}{5} + \frac{x}{8} + 10 + 1 = x$. The lowest common denominator is 120: so the equation now looks like this:

$\frac{40x}{120} + \frac{30x}{120} + \frac{24x}{120} + \frac{15x}{120} = x - 11$

$\frac{109x}{120} = x - 11$

$109x = 120x - 1{,}320$

$11x = 1{,}320$

$x = 120$

201. WILD & WOOLLY WORDY

One step forward, two steps back

202. DADDY DAY CARE

The Snowes have five, the Bialystocks four, the
Grossingers three, and the Sanchez family has two—fourteen kids in all. Knowing that each of the four families had
a different number of children, and that the total number
was less than eighteen, the first step was to factor 120
into four different numbers that together total less than
eighteen. The only possibility is two, three, four, and five—
which, when multiplied by each other, equal 120.

203. SEQUENTIAL THINKING

7. In each column, subtract the second number from the first (top) number and divide the result to get the bottom number: 16-2=14; 14÷2=7.

204. THIS OLD ANTIQUE

Mr. Pointelle, tea set, $1,000, 17th century

Mrs. Luce, serving tray, $800, 18th century

Ms. Bay, Venetian glass vase, $600, 19th century

205. SMUGGLER

All the previous cities hosted the Summer Olympic Games. The next city he'll show up in (if he isn't caught in the meantime) is London—in 2012.

206. ECHOES   Hoarse horse

207. PLAYING BY THE RULES

A large flightless bird with a long neck: Ostrich. According to the rules, a player describes an animal, and the next player has to think of an animal whose name begins with the letter the previous animal's name ended with. The sequence was: GiraffE, ElephanT, TigeR, RhinoceroS, SkunK, KangaroO...

208. LET'S GET PERSONAL

• Bree Winchell: Ramon on Monday; George on Wednesday, Thursday, and Friday

- Frieda Greenberg: Dmitri on Monday and Tuesday; Pietro on Wednesday and Thursday

- Maizie Nelson: George on Monday; Ramon on Tuesday, Wednesday, and Friday

- Ursula Bellini: George on Tuesday; Dmitri on Wednesday and Thursday; Pietro on Friday

- Terri Flaherty: Pietro on Monday and Tuesday; Ramon on Thursday; Dmitri on Friday

209. TRICKY, TRICKY

Neither would hit the ground first, because halfway during a transatlantic flight the plane would be over water.

210. GRADUATION DAY

Here's the configuration:

Buster	Rocky	Phoebe
Rosie	Max	Flossie
Jake	Molly	Bailey

From (clue 4) and (5), Rosie and Flossie can only appear in the second row in the first and third columns, respectively. From (2) and (4), Jake must be top left or bottom left, with Phoebe in the opposite corner. From (3) and (6), Buster can't be in the third column because then four dogs would be in that column (since Phoebe and Flossie are already there). So Buster is in the first column at the top left or bottom left, with Max and Rocky in the second column. From (2), Molly is also in the second column. So Bailey can only be in the remaining space in the third column. According to

(1), Bailey can't be at the top right because Max is in the row above. So Bailey is at the bottom right, Phoebe is at the top right, Jake is at the bottom left, Buster is at the top left with Rocky directly to the right. From (1), Max is in the center, leaving Molly in the middle of the bottom row.

211. SUPER SEVEN

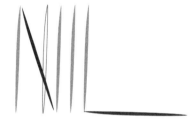

212. POLICE LINEUP

Number 2 robbed the jewelry store. The correct number of liars should yield only one culprit. If Number 1 were the perp, there was only one liar, the third eyewitness. If Number 3 were the culprit, then there was also only one liar: the first eyewitness. If Number 2 were the robber, then all three are lying. If there had been only one liar, the identity of the culprit would have been ambiguous, so there must have been three liars, with Number 2 being the guilty party.

213. THE CAT LADIES

The calicos are Alicia (owned by Bernice) and Denise (owned by Charlotte).

214. RIDDLER

They're both in the middle of waTer.

215. TWELVE SQUARE

There are several solutions. Here's ours:

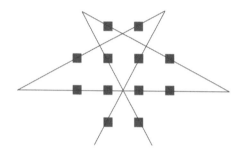

216. WHO OWNS THE ZEBRA?

The Norwegian drinks water, and the Japanese man owns the zebra.

House 1: yellow, Norwegian, water, Prius, fox

House 2: blue, Ukranian, tea, Lexus, horse

House 3: red, Englishman, milk, Hummer, snails

House 4: ivory, Spaniard, orange juice, Mercedes, dog

House 5: green, Japanese, coffee, Cadillac, zebra

217. THE AMAZING NUMBER 73

Entering a four-digit number twice, such as 36,243,624, is the same thing as multiplying it by 10,001. (3,624 x 10,001 = 36,243,624). Because 10,001 = 73 x 137, the eight-digit number will be divisible by 73, 137, and the original four-digit number.

218. WORD GAME

Our words are prince, princes, princess; and posse, posses, and possess. (But we think there might be a few more.)

219. I'LL HAVE WHAT HE'S HAVING

The second customer had placed $3:00 in change on the bar. The first customer had used three dollar bills.

220. PREFERENCES

Cancun. She only likes words whose first three letters are words: bag, top, etc.

221. THE MAGIC NUMBER SIX

$6 + 6/6 = 7$ or $6 + (6 \div 6) = 7$

222. LANGUAGE EQUATION 52 cards in a deck

223. QUICK TRICK

More people live in the United States than in Canada.

224. WILD & WOOLLY WORDY

Three blind mice (they have no I's).

225. HOURGLASS FIGURES

Start the 7- and 11-minute hourglasses when the pasta is dropped into the boiling water. When the sand runs out in the 7-minute hourglass, turn it over. When the sand runs out in the 11- minute hourglass, turn the 7-minute hourglass again. When the sand runs out again in the 7-minute hourglass, 15 minutes will have elapsed.

226. TO YOUR HEALTH

Christopher Weller, Acme Transport, jogs

Jerry Hurley, Pierre's French Laundry, bus

Stu Portnoy, Fizzy Cola bottling plant, bike

227. QUICK TRICK Downstream

228. THE COPS GET THEIR MAN

The plumber is the only man in the room; the other poker players are women.

229. ECHOES Banned band

230. THE ENGINE DRIVER BY BORIS KORDEMSKY (1900)

• The passenger who lives nearest the guard is not Petrov (d, e). He does not live in Moscow or Leningrad, since, at best, these are only tied for being nearest to the guard (b). So he is not Ivanov (a). By elimination he is Sidorov.

• Since the passenger from Leningrad is not Ivanov (a), by

elimination he is Petrov. The guard's name is Petrov (c). Since Sidorov is not the fireman (f), by elimination he is the engine driver.

231. TRIXIE'S KIDS

Knowing that their ages multiplied together equaled 36, the census taker knew their ages were one of these eight possibilities:

$$1 \times 1 \times 36 = 36$$
$$1 \times 2 \times 18 = 36$$
$$1 \times 3 \times 12 = 36$$
$$1 \times 4 \times 9 = 36$$
$$1 \times 6 \times 6 = 36$$
$$2 \times 2 \times 9 = 36$$
$$2 \times 3 \times 6 = 36$$
$$3 \times 3 \times 4 = 36$$

Each set of numbers added up equal the following totals:

$$1 + 1 + 36 = 38$$
$$1 + 2 + 18 = 21$$
$$1 + 3 + 12 = 16$$
$$1 + 4 + 9 = 14$$
$$1 + 6 + 6 = 13$$
$$2 + 2 + 9 = 13$$
$$2 + 3 + 6 = 11$$
$$3 + 3 + 4 = 10$$

Because 13 is the only sum with two possibilities, the census taker had to ask for another hint. (If the number on the house next door had been any of the other choices, the census taker wouldn't have needed a third hint.) So, the house number must have been 13. When Trixie said that tomorrow was her oldest child's birthday, the census taker ruled out the 1, 6, 6 combination because it has no largest number, and knew for certain that Trixie's kids were 2, 2, and 9 years old.

232. STICK IT

233. CASINO NIGHT
First: Olivia, craps, $30
Second: Bernadette, roulette, $20
Third: Carrie, bingo, $10
Fourth: Freddie, poker, $40
Fifth: Maribelle, blackjack, $50

234. LANGUAGE EQUATION
1,001 Arabian Nights

235. PUZZLING PEOPLE

Statement 4 is the only one that can be true, therefore:

Camilla: matchstick puzzles

Jeff: crosswords

Charles: math puzzles

Jillian: word-search puzzles

236. QUICK TRICK

$X = 4$; $Y = 11$. There are two alternating series: the first starts with the first number (7 6 5 4 3), the second starts with the second number (8 9 10 11 12).

237. SUPERHEROES

Since Jordan Green wasn't dressed as the Green Lantern and talked with Black Lightning, he must have been the Blue Devil. That leaves the Morgan Black wearing the BlueDevil costume, and Cameron Blue dressed as Black Lightning.

238. ECHOES Bizarre bazaar

239. GOT LOOT?

The man had been shipwrecked on a deserted island for four years; the chest he found was a pirate's treasure.

240. WORD LADDER Here's one way to do it: DEAD, LEAD, LEND, LAND, LANE, LINE, LIVE.

241. THE NIGHT SHIFT

The watchman had obviously been sleeping on the job.

242. AT HOME WITH THE WELLOFFS

Monday: Mrs. Welloff holds a séance.

Tuesday: Jessica the maid helps move a piano.

Wednesday: Kristina the cook has a run-in with a used-car salesman.

Thursday: Bob the chauffeur joins a karaoke club.

Friday: Mr. Welloff gets locked in the meat freezer.

243. LETTER PERFECT

In this sentence there are four R's, five T's, and two V's.

244. ECHOES

Sights sites

245. WHAT DO YOU THINK?

There are more 2s. Every number from 20,000 to 29,999 begins with a 2. The 8s wouldn't begin to catch up until well into the 80,000s.

246. CAREFUL WHAT YOU WISH FOR

Jim told the genie, "I wish that my father could see his granddaughter lying in a diamond-encrusted bassinet."

247. AT THE STORE

Produce is on aisle 1, cereal on aisle 2, cleaning products on aisle 3, beverages on aisle 4, meat on aisle 5, and bread on aisle 6.

248. NOT YOUR GRANDDAD'S CRYPTOGRAM

The decoded message: The first letter is advanced by one position, the second letter by two positions, and so on.

249. SIBLING RIVALRY

Three sisters and two brothers.

250. MOMMY'S LITTLE GIRL

The mother is 40 and the daughter is 10.

251. CAPITAL PUN-ISHMENT   beer belly

252. THE THREE SISTERS

Dorothy is 6, Christine is 9, and Phyllis is 20.

253. LANGUAGE EQUATION

26 letters in the alphabet

254. TURN THAT FROWN UPSIDE DOWN

Here's one way to do it: TEARS, SEARS, STARS, STARE, STALE, STILE, SMILE.

255. ANAGRAM THIS

1. They see

2. Lies, let's recount

256. PICK A NUMBER, ANY NUMBER

How it works: 9 x 12,345,679 = 111,111,111, so when your person multiplies his number by both those numbers, he's multiplying it by 111,111,111.

257. TEASER

None. You're thinking of Noah, not Moses.

258. THE CHECK'S IN THE MAIL

Here's one way to do it: BLANK, BLINK, CLINK, CLICK, CHICK, CHECK.

259. IT'S A BARGAIN

House numbers. A "1" costs $5, and so does a "2." A "12" consists of a 1 and a 2 so you'll have to buy two numbers at $5 each. A "144" consists of three numbers, which costs $15.

260. QUICK TRICK

Write 12 in Roman numerals: XII. Then divide the number in half horizontally. The upper half is VII.

261. WHISTLESTOP WHEELS

First Street: Edith Westwood off, Xavier Merkowitz on
Second Street: Yolanda French off, John Vanderbeer on
Third Street: Vincent Ulrich off, Honey Graham on
Fourth Street: Hilda Robertson off, Frances Orwell on
Bernice Costa rode all the way from Morris Avenue to the
very last stop.

262. BEST IN SHOW

Dogs' Names: Arfur, Ruff, Woof, Yip-yip
Handlers' Names: Bill, June, Ruth, Terence
Classes: Novice, Open, Puppy, Senior
Breeds: Cockapoo, Giant Schnoodle, Labradoodle, Yorkipoo

Dog	Handler	Class	Place	Breed
Woof	June	Senior	3rd	Cockapoo
Arfur	Bill	Puppy	1st	Labradoodle
Ruff	Ruth	Novice	4th	Giant Schnoodle
Yip-yip	Terence	Open	9th	Yorkipoo

263. IT'S A LIVING

Alfie is the architect, Buford is the dentist, Cedric is the
caseworker, and Raymond is the barber.

264. PLAYING CARDS

There are two possible solutions.

265. WILD & WOOLLY WORDY

A play on words

266. ECHOES Minor miner

267. THE MARRYING KIND

1978: Stan, Beijing, 20

1985: Jorge, London, 18

1991: Abel, Los Angeles, 22

1996: Marco, Venice, 23

2000: Donald, New York, 19

268. THE SIGN SAYS?

10 miles (five miles for each vowel)

269. BLACK HATS VS. WHITE HATS

If any of the three previous students had said their hat was black, that would mean that the other three (including the fourth student) were all wearing white hats. But none of them did, which means that they all saw both black and white hats on the others. The fourth student must have seen three white hats; that's the only way she would know that her hat was black.

270. FERTILE FIELDS

Here's one way to do it: WHEAT, CHEAT, CHEAP, CHEEP, CREEP, CREED, BREED, BREAD.

271. NUMBER PROBLEM

A decimal point (3.7)

272. YES DICE

Have I rolled a YES?

273. WILD & WOOLLY WORDY

Water (H to O = H_2O)

274. TEASERS

1. 16 (Two pairs of twins are eight.)

2. The 25th

275. TRIANGULATE THIS

276. FIGURE IT OUT

Fill the three-gallon jug, and empty the contents into the five-gallon jug. Then fill the three-gallon jug again, and use this to fill the five-gallon jug until it's full. You'll end up with one gallon left in the three-gallon jug.

277. QUICK TRICK

15. It's the only number that isn't a prime number.

278. SCAPEGOAT

Here's one way to do it: SHIFT, SHIRT, SHIRE, SHARE, SHAKE, SLAKE, FLAKE, FLAME, BLAME.

279. ROBBERY ON THE ORIENT EXPRESS

Roberto de Starz robbed the four passengers as follows:
Princess Ann of Monglovia in the baggage car, $10,000
Friedrich Von Monocle in the sleeper car, $7,500
Doctor Humphrey Fahrquar in the dining car, $5,000
Madame Sheeza Tutzibelle in the passenger car, $2,500

280. SMOOCHY STRIKES AGAIN

Here's one way to do it: KISS, MISS, MOSS, LOSS, LOSE, LOVE.

281. AND THE NUMBER IS?

155. Consecutive numbers are multiplied together and 1 is added to the answer. $1 \times 1 + 1 = 2$; $1 \times 2 + 1 = 3$; $2 \times 3 + 1 = 7$; $3 \times 7 + 1 = 22$; $7 \times 22 = 154 + 1 = 155$.

282. LONG LIVE THE EMPEROR!

He was 79 years old (there was no year zero).

283. SEQUENTIAL THINKING

49. The numbers are squares of 3, 4, 5, 6, and 7

284. ON YOUR MARK...

Six

285. WONDERFUL WORDPLAY

Intense, diffuse

286. THE "IGOTCHA" DIAMOND

The diamond must be in the gold box; otherwise all the inscriptions would be either true or false.

287. RIDDLE ME THIS

1. The word "ton"

2. Eileen (I lean)

3. A library—because it has the most stories

288. HAIR TODAY, A CLASSIC

You should pick the first shop. Since there are only two barbers in town, each must have cut the other's hair. The wisest choice would be the barber who had given his rival the best haircut.

289. WILD & WOOLLY WORDY A walk in the park

290. CIRCLES SQUARED

Puzzle #1

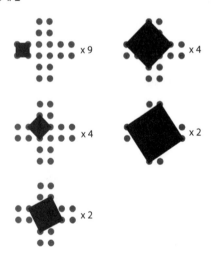

Puzzle #2

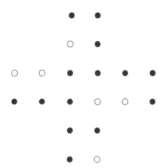

291. DIGITS
194

292. TEASER
They are not playing each other.

293. WONDERFUL WORDPLAY
The tricky answer is "soap." Turn the "b" upside down and backward to turn it into a "p."

294. QUICK TRICK
Push the cork into the bottle, then tip the bottle upside down and remove the coin.

295. AND THE NUMBER IS?

1,595. Reverse each set of digits and add the result to the original number to make the next number: 31 + 13 = 44; 44 + 44 = 88; 88 + 88 = 176; 671 + 176 = 847; 748 + 847 = 1595.

296. IT WAS HERE A MINUTE AGO...

Here's one way to do it: LOST, LIST, LINT, LINE, FINE, FIND.

297. ECHOES

Birth berth

298. ONE BIG HAPPY FAMILY

Seven: two little girls, a boy, their parents, and their father's parents.

299. ROOM FOR IMPROVEMENT

Here's one way to do it: FAIL, PAIL, PALL, PALS, PASS.

300. A MOTHER'S LOVE

When Sir Flushalot pulled a slip of paper from the bowl, he read it and declared "I've won!" Then he ate the paper. The remaining piece of paper said "The Snakes," and the queen's trickery was never revealed.

301. SEQUENTIAL THINKING

145. After subtracting one from each number, multiply by 3 going down and 2 going across.

302. FACE TIME

Twenty hours later, the faster clock was ahead by one hour. With every passing hour, the quicker clock gained three minutes on the slower one. (3 minutes per hour x 20 hours = 60 minutes, or one hour.)

303. ECHOES Dear deer

304. TRICKY

His age—he'd be about 150 years old.

305. FLYING HIGH

The balloon moves forward. When the bus moves forward, the air moves to the back of bus. The helium balloon, though, is lighter than air, so it's pushed forward.

306. WHEN IN ROME...

V. The letters are from a watch or clock face that uses Roman numerals, reading clockwise from 9:00 (IX).

307. HOMOPHONE

I was so poor that it didn't make any SENSE to spend 99 CENTS on the SCENTS at the perfume shop.

308. NOBODY'S FOOL

Here's one way to do it: FOOL, POOL, POLL, PALL, PALE, PAGE, SAGE.

309. CAPITAL PUN-ISHMENT

Electric bill

310. WILD & WOOLLY WORDY

Painless operation

311. RUSHED TO THE HOSPITAL

The wearing of seat belts was successful in reducing the number of deaths from road accidents. The accident victims who wore seat belts ended up at the hospital instead of the morgue. Consequently, more people were treated for injuries than before.

312. ECHOES

Pale pail

313. GRIDDY NUMBERS

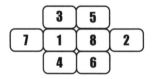

314. INSPECTOR LOO SNIFFS OUT AN ANSWER

He smelled Old Spice on them.

It seems the robbers ran out of the jewelry store, dashed into the alley, and hid behind a dumpster as they whipped off their black clothing and masks. Underneath, they had shaved heads and monks' garb, attire they believed would remove them from all suspicion. The police recovered the loot in the dumpster, where the robbers had stashed it with plans to return for it later, once things calmed down.

315. THE LOST LETTER

F for February. The letters are the initials of the first eight months of the year.

316. DOUBLE TIME

1. By continuously removing one letter from either the beginning or the end of each word, you create new words until you're left with just the letter "a."

        Sheath, heath, heat, eat, at, a

        Pirate, irate, rate, ate, at, a

        Ashamed, shamed, shame, sham, ham, am, a

        Brandy, brand, bran, ran, an, a

2. Stench. All of the other words can be used as both nouns and verbs, but stench can be used only as a noun.

317. GREEN, GREEN GRASS
Here's one way to do it. GRASS, CRASS, CRESS, TRESS, TREES, TREED, GREED, GREEN.

318. HOMOPHONE
If the cut on Jason's HEEL doesn't HEAL in time for the big race, HE'LL just have to watch from the sidelines.

319. RIDDLERS
1. A stamp   **2.** A river

320. TRICKY, TRICKY
"Chore" and "heat" are anagrams of "each other."

321. QUICK TRICK
8. There are two alternating series, both of which start with zero. The first is 0, 1, 2, 3, 4; the second is 0, 2, 4, 6.

322. DOUBLE-SPEAK
1. Every cloud has a silver lining.
2. Haste makes waste.
3. Too many cooks spoil the broth.
4. A rolling stone gathers no moss.
5. Silence is golden.

323. THE MISSING LETTER
The letter O. The phrase is "To be, or not to be."

324. HELLO? HELLO?

First: Janelle called her friend Bella.

Second: Renee called the Pizza Palace.

Third: Matilda called the beauty supply store.

Fourth: April called the dentist.

Fifth: Nadia called her mother.

325. ONE OF A KIND.

It contains all the digits in alphabetical order.

326. TRICKY MATH

Add a line to one of the plus signs to make a 4.

327. QUICK TRICK

Draw a line of over the second 1 so that it now reads "10 TO 10."

328. WHAT'S THE WORD   Eye

329. WORD LADDER

Here's one way to do it: RIVER, ROVER, COVER, COVES, CORES, CORNS, COINS, CHINS, SHINS, SHINE, SHONE, SHORE.

330. A DEATH IN THE FAMILY

Dick and Jane were goldfish. The family dog was the culprit. Labs have powerful tails, and his inadvertently swept the fishbowl onto the floor when he passed by the table on which it rested.

331. HERE FISHY, FISHY

332. LET'S GET DIVISIVE
The two numbers are 44 and 66.

333. FIND THE COUNTERFEIT
1. The first two operations are to weigh coins 1, 2, 3, and 4 against 5, 6, 7, and 8; then to weigh coins 9, 10, 11, and 4 against 1, 2, 3, and 8.

2. If the scales balance in both cases, 12 must be the counterfeit coin.

3. If the scales balanced in the first weighing but not in the second, weigh coin 9 against coin 10 to see which tips the same way as in the second weighing. If they balance, 11 is the counterfeit.

4. If the scales balance in the second weighing but not in the first, weigh coin 5 against coin 6 to see which tips in the same way as in the first weighing. If they balance, 7 is the counterfeit.

5. If the scales are off-balance the same way both times, weigh coin 5 against another coin. If they balance, the counterfeit is 8.

6. If the scales are off-balance in opposite ways in the first two weighings, weigh coin 1 against coin 2 to see which tips as 1, 2, and 3 tipped in the second weighing. If they balance, 3 is the counterfeit coin.

334. LETTER PLAY
Above the line. All the letters up there hang down when in lower case: g, j, q, y, and p.

335. ANAGRAM THIS
Teachers, cheaters

336. RIDDLER
Pants

337. FEEDING TIME
Cats, 8:30 a.m.; birds, 8:45 a.m.; fish, 9:00 a.m.; puppies, 9:15 a.m.; snakes, 7:30 a.m.

338. WHO SNATCHED MRS. MURGATROYD'S PURSE?

Bluto did it. Based on the considerations that two of the three witnesses made no true statements and that the truthfulness of the third witness is unknown, we can start by assuming that A's claim that Gus is guilty is true. If so, two of A's statements are true, none of B's statements are true, and one of C's statements is true. Therefore, Gus did not do it. Bluto must have.

339. WILD & WOOLLY WORDY

No U-turn

340. BARBERSHOP QUIZTET

Just as you see it. The mirror reverses the word, but looking at it from the other side of the window reverses it back.

341. NATURAL RESOURCES

Here's one way to do it: OIL, NIL, NIP, NAP, GAP, GAS.

342. TEASER Stop imagining!

343. NUMBERS IN A SEQUENCE

a. (9 1). There are two series, one starting with 10 and going down one number each time, and one starting with 1 and going up one number. Or you could look at the number as a palindrome, i.e., reading the same forward and back, with the two 5s as the center of the palindrome. (In which case a 10 would follow the 9 1.)

344. LANGUAGE EQUATION

365 days in a year

345. WONDERFUL WORDPLAY

Athletes. He only likes words that start with prepositions.

346. THE HIDDEN MESSAGE

Take the fifth word, then count six and take the next word, then count seven and take the next word, and so on to reveal the message "The supplies will arrive early Tuesday morning."

347. AND THE NUMBER IS?

6. The sum of the numbers reading down in each column increases by two.

6 + 3 + 4 + 5 = 18

4 + 5 + 7 + 4 = 20

8 + 3 + 4 + 7 = 22

3 + 9 + 6 + 6 = 24

348. TAKING THE TOUR

The tourist on the two-hour boat sees all the boats going the other way around that left up to three hours previously or that will leave in the next two hours. The tourist on the three-hour boat sees all the boats going the other way that left up to two hours previously or that will leave in the next three hours. In five hours, including the beginning and the end, 21 boats depart in each direction. Including the boats on which they are traveling, each tourist therefore sees 22 boats on the trip.

349. COLOR COORDINATION

164. By assigning numbers to the letters as they appear in the alphabet (A = 1, B = 2, C = 3, etc.), yellow (92) plus black (39) will equal 131.

350. EUREKA!

Here's one way to do it: ROCK, ROOK, HOOK, HOOD, GOOD, GOLD.

351. WILD & WOOLLY WORDY

Tuna fish (2 NA FISH)

352. MURDER AT THE B&B

11:45 p.m. She saw a mirror image of the clock face.

353. UPHILL AND DOWNHILL: A CLASSIC PUZZLE BY LEWIS CARROLL

A level mile takes 15 minutes to walk, an uphill mile takes 20 minutes, and a downhill mile 10 minutes. So to go and return over the same mile, whether on the level or on the hillside, takes half an hour. Hence, in 6 hours they went 12 miles out and 12 miles back. If the 12 miles out had been nearly all level, they would have taken a little over 3 hours; if nearly all uphill, a little under 4 hours. Hence,

3½ hours must be within half an hour of the time taken in reaching the peak; thus, as they started at 3:00, they got there within half an hour of half past 6:00.

354. CALENDAR DAZE

1. The 15th

2. The 25th

3. The 7th

4. Four

5. The 27th

355. GOING GREEK MUSE

356. LIKE CLOCKWORK

The answer is 11 times. Every hour, they meet about five minutes later than the previous hour. Starting at noon, the next times they'll meet are 1:08, 2:10, 3:16, 4:21, 5:27, 6:32, 7:38, 8:43, 9:49, 10:54, and 12:00.

357. WHAT'S THE WORD? Giggle

358. QUICK ID

The criminal was Cecil. The order from front to back: Gerhard, Hank, Bruce, Cecil, Ernesto, Drew, Dennis, Fats.

359. UNSCRAMBLE IT

BEZIQUES

360. LANGUAGE EQUATION
Seven Wonders of the World

361. BAG OF TRICKS
The chest that's labeled ONE OF EACH is intentionally mislabeled, so you know it either contains two bags of dollars or two bags of doughnuts. This is the chest you should open. If the bag you open inside it contains dollars, that's the chest to choose. If the bag contains doughnuts, this chest contains all doughnuts, and you should choose the box that's mislabeled DOUGHNUTS. That's where the two bags of dollars will be.

362. WORD LADDER
Here's one way to do it: EAST, LAST, LUST, DUST, DUET, DUES, DYES, EYES, EVES, EVEN, EDEN.

363. BOOK LEARNIN'
The man was returning an overdue library book.

364. TEASERS
1. He weighs meat.
2. You'd rather the crocodile attacked the alligator, wouldn't you?

365. TRICKY, TRICKY
Both "stifle" and "filets" are anagrams of "itself."

UNCLE JOHN'S BATHROOM PUZZLERS: FOR PUZZLE LOVERS

Find these and other great *Uncle John's Bathroom Reader* titles online at www.bathroomreader.com.

Or contact us:
Bathroom Readers' Institute
PO Box 1117
Ashland, OR 97520
(888) 488-4642

Also available from the Bathroom Readers' Institute…

Test your friends…test yourself! *Uncle John's Bathroom Reader Ultimate Challenge Trivia Quiz* and *Uncle John's Did You Know* are packed with fun, fascinating facts.

Bathroom Readers' Institute
PO Box 1117
Ashland, OR 97520
www.bathroomreader.com